A JOURNEY
from the
BEGINNING

*Other Books by Margaret Ghosn
published by Coventry Press*

The Miracle of Love
Samaritan Journey

CREATION ACCOUNTS
IN THE BOOK OF GENESIS

A JOURNEY *from the* BEGINNING

—— MARGARET GHOSN ——

COVENTRY PRESS

Published in Australia by
Coventry Press
33 Scoresby Road
Bayswater VIC 3153

ISBN 9781922589149

Copyright © Margaret Ghosn 2022

All rights reserved. Other than for the purposes and subject to the conditions prescribed under the *Copyright Act*, no part of this publication may be reproduced, stored in a retrieval system, or transmitted in any form or by any means, electronic, mechanical, photocopying, recording or otherwise, without the prior permission of the publisher.

Scripture quotations are from the *New Revised Standard Version Bible*, copyright 1989, Division of Christian Education of the National Council of the Churches of Christ in the United States of America. Used by permission. All rights reserved.

Catalogue-in-Publication entry is available from the National Library of Australia http://catalogue.nla.gov.au

Cover design by Ian James – www.jgd.com.au
Text design by Coventry Press
Set in Tex Gyre Pagella (Palatino)

Printed in Australia

Contents

Introduction 7

Chapter 1   Let's start at the very beginning 11

Chapter 2   There is a wonderful world 29

Chapter 3   With people 49

Chapter 4   Life is a blessing 63

Chapter 5   Be co-creators 74

Chapter 6   For we are not alone 102

Chapter 7   Despite troubles 120

Chapter 8   We can begin again 163

Bibliography 194

Introduction

Sometimes writings about Christ or biblical reflections seem outdated. People today have other interests. Their phones do all the talking and thinking for them. Games matter. Tik Tok matters. The focus is on technology at our fingertips. And then there are the real world issues we are facing – electoral fraud, political unrest, world powers on edge, false news, gender fluidity, culture cancel, media dictatorship, algorithmic use of social media accounts etc.

So why write about God? Why even refer to the Bible when Google has all the answers? Perhaps, despite the myriad of possibilities at our fingertips, we are still uneasy about living in a godless world.

People still search for meaning and goodness. They want to live lives of worth and to be responsible in the face of corruption, power abuse and unbridled technology. They want to continue to live out the truth that God matters, and is necessary.

This book focuses on the first three chapters of the Book of Genesis which seeks to answer some of life's basic questions that in today's world have become ever more pertinent. The Book of Genesis is a book of aetiologies – stories explaining the origins of things – and is divided into three parts:

Part I   Primeval History (1-11)
Part II   Patriarchal History (12-36)

- Abraham (12:1 to 25:18)
- Isaac (25:19 to 26:35)
- Jacob (27:1 to 37:1)

Part III   Story of Joseph (37:2 to 50:26)

Genesis chapter 1 comes from the time of the exile of Israel in Babylon (586-538 BCE) when the people needed to understand that God was Creator, who ordered all things, and that every day was holy. This encouraged the people to remain with God, even though they were in a foreign land surrounded by false gods. Our world today is no different with the lure of the world competing with fidelity to God.

There are two different creation accounts in the Book of Genesis. We have Genesis 1:1 to 2:3 which concerns the cosmic plan of creation, and Genesis 2:4-25 that focuses attention on humans as the cultivator of their environment.

We also have two accounts of the creation of humans. Genesis 1:26-29 emphasises humanity made 'in the image' of God; and Genesis 2:7-8, 15-25 presents humans created from 'the dust of the earth' and functioning in partnership. Chapter three puts forward humans as moral agents, suggesting a backstory to how things in human life and society have come to be the way they are. These accounts are metaphorically interpreted and emphasise the theological message of God's relationship with humanity.

The three chapters will be studied theologically, while conversing with other disciplines, as the biblical texts in

INTRODUCTION

Genesis involve historical, literary and linguistic processes. It impacts on our lives socially, psychologically and emotionally. As William P. Brown, notes:

> It is critical to recognize that Scripture itself is the product of a community, the work of a people whose identity was shaped by the exigencies of history, on the one hand, and an abiding conviction of divine providence, on the other... As the ancient community of faith played an active role in the formation of Scripture, so contemporary communities of faith must never cease in actively interpreting Scripture so that the Word made flesh remains fresh. Indeed, such critical reflection is necessarily self-reflective: the ancient contexts of biblical tradition help to highlight our contemporary contexts as readers.[1]

Aside from a study of the texts, the following pages will allow the spirit of Creation, that is also the spirit within each one of us, to lead us on this journey of cosmic beginnings and our own personal journey. With all this in mind, we will take a closer look at the first three chapters of Genesis to see what they reveal to us in our contemporary times and how the Bible still has a necessary contribution to make in our lives, personally and communally, while living in this technological age.

---

[1] William P. Brown, 'From Apology to Pedagogy: Interpreting the Bible Past and Present in the Seminary Classroom' in *A Journal of Bible and Theology* 66(4), 2012: 378.

Chapter 1

Let's start at the very beginning

The Bible's first words introduce us to the world, its very beginning and evolution. We are warmly welcomed to this world by God. This is our place, our home and everything belongs.

1 *In the beginning when God created the heavens and the earth, ^{2} the earth was a formless void and darkness covered the face of the deep, while a wind from God swept over the face of the waters. ^{3} Then God said, 'Let there be light'; and there was light. ^{4} And God saw that the light was good; and God separated the light from the darkness. ^{5} God called the light Day, and the darkness he called Night. And there was evening and there was morning, the first day.*
^{6} And God said, 'Let there be a dome in the midst of the waters, and let it separate the waters from the waters.' ^{7} So God made the dome and separated the waters that were under the dome from the waters that were above the dome. And it was so. ^{8} God called the dome Sky. And there was evening and there was morning, the second day.
^{9} And God said, 'Let the waters under the sky be gathered together into one place, and let the dry land appear.' And it was so. ^{10} God called the dry land Earth, and the waters

that were gathered together he called Seas. And God saw that it was good. ¹¹Then God said, 'Let the earth put forth vegetation: plants yielding seed, and fruit trees of every kind on earth that bear fruit with the seed in it.' And it was so. ¹²The earth brought forth vegetation: plants yielding seed of every kind, and trees of every kind bearing fruit with the seed in it. And God saw that it was good. ¹³And there was evening and there was morning, the third day.

¹⁴And God said, 'Let there be lights in the dome of the sky to separate the day from the night; and let them be for signs and for seasons and for days and years, ¹⁵and let them be lights in the dome of the sky to give light upon the earth.' And it was so. ¹⁶God made the two great lights—the greater light to rule the day and the lesser light to rule the night—and the stars. ¹⁷God set them in the dome of the sky to give light upon the earth, ¹⁸to rule over the day and over the night, and to separate the light from the darkness. And God saw that it was good. ¹⁹And there was evening and there was morning, the fourth day.

²⁰And God said, 'Let the waters bring forth swarms of living creatures, and let birds fly above the earth across the dome of the sky.' ²¹So God created the great sea monsters and every living creature that moves, of every kind, with which the waters swarm, and every winged bird of every kind. And God saw that it was good. ²²God blessed them, saying, 'Be fruitful and multiply and fill the waters in the seas, and let birds multiply on the earth.' ²³And there was evening and there was morning, the fifth day.

²⁴And God said, 'Let the earth bring forth living creatures of every kind: cattle and creeping things and wild animals of the earth of every kind.' And it was so. ²⁵God made the wild animals of the earth of every kind, and the cattle of

every kind, and everything that creeps upon the ground of every kind. And God saw that it was good. ²⁶*Then God said, 'Let us make humankind in our image, according to our likeness; and let them have dominion over the fish of the sea, and over the birds of the air, and over the cattle, and over all the wild animals of the earth, and over every creeping thing that creeps upon the earth.'*

²⁷*So God created humankind in his image,*
in the image of God he created them;
male and female he created them.

²⁸*God blessed them, and God said to them, 'Be fruitful and multiply, and fill the earth and subdue it; and have dominion over the fish of the sea and over the birds of the air and over every living thing that moves upon the earth.'* ²⁹*God said, 'See, I have given you every plant yielding seed that is upon the face of all the earth, and every tree with seed in its fruit; you shall have them for food.* ³⁰*And to every beast of the earth, and to every bird of the air, and to everything that creeps on the earth, everything that has the breath of life, I have given every green plant for food.' And it was so.* ³¹*God saw everything that he had made, and indeed, it was very good. And there was evening and there was morning, the sixth day.*

2 *Thus the heavens and the earth were finished, and all their multitude.* ²*And on the seventh day God finished the work that he had done, and he rested on the seventh day from all the work that he had done.* ³*So God blessed the seventh day and hallowed it, because on it God rested from all the work that he had done in creation.*

⁴*These are the generations of the heavens and the earth when they were created.*

Genesis 1:1 to 2:4a

The first chapter of Genesis speaks to our time and place. It speaks the word on creation and evolution, on our solar system and Earth, on all its diverse creatures and humanity. Let us return to the beginning, picture the past, the history that has unfurled, so that upon returning to the here and now, we will continue on with the story of creating.

In the beginning... there is a story to tell. There is always a beginning and from the beginning there emerges other beginnings. In the beginning, there was promise and the fulfilment takes a lifetime. The beginning sets the stage for the imagination to work, holding possibilities, a canvas to be painted upon, heightening enthusiasm. What will happen in this new venture?

> **Genesis 1:1-2** *In the beginning when God created the heavens and the earth, ^{2} the earth was a formless void and darkness covered the face of the deep, while a wind from God swept over the face of the waters.*

The beginning is a formless void. Our universe is dark, quiet, empty and silent. It is in the darkness, silence, emptiness, where the stirrings of life commence. Just like the beginnings of human life, formed in the darkness of the mother's womb.

In the darkness, in the deep, something is hidden, beyond our sight. All things start undefined, unnoticeable, in shadows, unknown. Mystery stirs, awaiting the dawn of day, so as to burst into life.

'In the beginning when God created' reads Genesis 1:1. It is a divine beginning. The beginning is God's time. What emerges appears out of desire, hope and love. A journey has begun. The Bible opens with the birth of the universe by the Creator of all. Yet although God introduces everything, God is not introduced, because God is before all things. A God who introduces us to this world.

> Before the mountains were brought forth, or ever you had formed the earth and the world, from everlasting to everlasting you are God.
>
> Psalm 90:2

The Bible offers us a number of accounts of creation. These include:

- Genesis 1:1 to 2:4a

- Genesis 2:4b to 3:24

- Job 38 to 41

- Psalm 104: humans and all living creatures exercise their right to live in God's world. The psalmist and God delight in the variety of creatures and habitats that fill creation. The Psalm is God's fanfare for the common creature.

- Psalms 74:12-17

- Proverbs 8:22-31: Wisdom is a form of loving knowledge that involves humility and wonder before the natural world and recognises human finitude before the mystery of God and creation.

> My hand laid the foundation of the earth,
>   and my right hand spread out the heavens;
> when I summon them, they stand at attention.
>
> Isaiah 48:13

> Thus says the LORD, your Redeemer,
>   who formed you in the womb:
> I am the LORD, who made all things,
>   who alone stretched out the heavens,
>   who by myself spread out the earth.
>
> Isaiah 44:24

Such biblical passages claim the world as God's creation and acknowledge creation's worth and integrity, goodness and beauty. Creation bears the semblance of God, touched with creativity and blessed with beauty. Brian Swimme and Thomas Berry write:

> Originating power brought forth a universe... all the energy that would ever exist in the entire course of time erupted as a single quantum – a singular gift – existence ... In the beginning space foamed forth to create the vast billowing event of the expanding universe. The universe venture was under way.[2]

The Sumerians, Babylonians, Egyptians and Greeks described the beginning of the world as one great primal sea.

- Among the Greeks, Okeanos was the father of all the gods and was depicted as a bull-horned god with the tail of a serpentine fish
- The Assyrians described how the waters above and beneath were there before the heaven and earth had their names

---

[2] Brian Swimme and Thomas Berry, *The Universe Story: From the Primordial Flaring Forth to the Ecozoic Era - A Celebration of the Unfolding of the Cosmos*, (San Francisco: HarperSanFrancisco, 1992).

- The Canaanites believed the creator god Baal vanquished the primordial sea deity Yam, a male god, and formed the seas and the sky from its remains
- In the Babylonian Epic of Creation, *Enuma Elish*, 'all lands were still sea'. It describes creation happening after the male god Marduk kills the female god Tiamat, then tears her body apart, using half of her to create the heavens and half to create the earth.

Yet our story differs in a radical way. Our journey begins with wonder. Genesis 1 has one God, who creates not from war and vengeance. When God creates, it is through generous love, as Pope Francis aptly describes.

> The beginning of the world was not a work of chaos that owes its origin to another but derives directly from a supreme Principle who creates out of love. The Big Bang theory, which is proposed today as the origin of the world, does not contradict the intervention of a divine creator but depends on it. Evolution in nature does not conflict with the notion of Creation, because evolution presupposes the creation of beings who evolve.[3]

---

[3] Pope Francis, Plenary Session of The Pontifical Academy of Sciences. Address of His Holiness Pope Francis on The Occasion of The Inauguration of The Bust in Honour Of Pope Benedict XVI Monday, 27 October 2014. https://w2.vatican.va/content/francesco/en/speeches/2014/october/documents/papa-francesco_20141027_plenaria-accademia-scienze.html

Creation is *ex nihilo*, out of nothing, but God's creative grace makes fertile the empty space. It is the spirit of God pulsating and awakening life with its grandeur and endless marvel.

In Genesis 1:2 we read, 'The earth was a formless void and darkness covered the face of the deep, while a wind from God swept over the face of the waters'. God starts a new venture creating out of love, birthing, brewing, caressing, coaxing, colouring, designing, developing, disrupting, diversifying, encouraging, enticing, fashioning, forging, imagining, moulding, nurturing, patterning, piecing, planting, shaping, tossing, turning, unfolding, watering and weaving. A world of all possibilities. Again, Pope Francis puts it wonderfully, 'Our God is not inert, but our God – allow me to say – is a dreamer'.[4]

Margaret Silf writes that there is God's Spirit, energy, sweeping, erupting and foaming forth. I look inside myself, especially when I am in the midst of flux and change, and I see: formlessness, emptiness, darkness, depth, tossing and churning. What might happen with this raw material if I could let the Spirit hover? A wind of change and transformation can blow across the dark void; a new energy can emerge or even erupt; new possibilities can 'foam forth' one by one, instant by instant; this is the singular gift of existence, forever renewing itself.[5]

---

[4] Pope Francis, General Audience, Wednesday, 17 May 2017. http://w2.vatican.va/content/francesco/en/audiences/2017/documents/papa-francesco_20170517_udienza-generale.html

[5] Margaret Silf, *The other side of chaos. Breaking through when life is breaking down*, (Chicago: Loyola Press, 2011), 44.

This Spirit is what we read about at the beginning of Scripture, when 'a wind from God swept over the face of the waters' and creation began. The Spirit of life comes when there is 'formless void and darkness' (1:2). Life becomes animated and God's imaginative Holy Spirit designs flamboyantly. We throb with creation. We pulsate with energy. The journey of life is enticing. As Seamus Heaney describes it, we feel, 'Unroofed scope. Knowledge-freshening wind'.[6]

God's creation of the universe took place through the presence of the Holy Spirit, that wind that swept over the face of the waters. Jesus' ministry begins at baptism, when the Holy Spirit descended upon him in the form of a dove. The Spirit at the beginning of God's creation appears again as wind when the disciples 'were altogether in one place' (Acts 2:1), huddled in fear and uncertainty. The Spirit bursts in, scatters the darkness and apprehension, tossing everything into new life.

> And suddenly from heaven there came a sound like the rush of a violent wind, and it filled the entire house.
>
> Acts 2:2

It is a Spirit that comes into our depths, our times of fear and trepidation, to offer a new lease on life. It is elusive but present, everywhere but hidden. It can neither be tamed nor contained. Spirit is about allowing the unexpected to happen, the freedom to be, the openness to ever more wider vistas.

---

[6] Seamus Heaney, 'Lightenings,' in *Seeing Things*, (London: Faber, 2010).

The world is a call to spirituality. It is about mystery, soaring to new heights, wide-eyed wonder, but also a life of action, determination, creativity and mission. The Spirit is at the heart of creation. It is part of this world and we are immersed in the Spirit of God. A Spirit of energy and love, always present, stirring up and recreating.

> The wind blows where it chooses and you hear the sound of it, but you do not know where it comes from or where it goes. So it is with everyone who is born of the Spirit.
>
> John 3:8

A wind that sweeps by and brushes everything with colour, blowing here and there. Jane N. Dowling notes that when we pray, the Spirit makes 'a noise' within us as we begin to experience subtle and obvious movements within, including sadness dissipating, discouragement scampering, as new courage emerges, hope arising, doubts evaporating before renewed faith that rains upon us. We hear within ourselves the subtle sound of distant music until we experience the gift of being restored spiritually to life through the 'breath' that is Spirit.[7]

'A wind from God swept over the face of the waters.' To sweep is to unsettle the dust, stir things up, create order out of chaos. Coming unexpectedly, God's Spirit arouses anticipation in us. Like God, can we take one sweeping glance and envision a future? To sweep is to prepare for the revealing of new things. The wind from God swept, and

---

[7] Jane N. Dowling, *Come Forward! Bold enough to heal. A Spiritual Handbook for survivors of sexual abuse using Scripture, Visualisation and Art Therapy*, (Victoria, Australia: Coventry Press, 2019), 80

we too are swept away with wonder; dust and cobwebs are removed, emotions are stirred and our depths are moved. Creating is to reveal what has been hidden. In our journey of life, we are enticed out of waters of darkness into a new being of light, to be 'born of water and Spirit' (John 3:5).

The first thing that God does in creation is to speak (1:3, 6, 9, 14, 20, 24, 26, 28, 29) and God does so a number of times. And what does God say...

> **Genesis 1:3-5** *Then God said, 'Let there be light'; and there was light. ⁴And God saw that the light was good; and God separated the light from the darkness. ⁵God called the light Day, and the darkness he called Night. And there was evening and there was morning, the first day.*

'Then God said.' The first stage of creation begins with the creative word, the idea, the vision, the dream. Language lies at the heart of our uniqueness as the image of God as Rabbi Jonathan Sacks notes. Just as God makes the natural world by words, so we make the human world by words. God is revealed to humanity in and through sacred words.[8]

To speak is to allow light to enter darkness and transform it. God speaks words that create a new vision out of darkness. The power of words can create and bring to light.

God's wind and word animate life. God wills that there should be light and life. That colour brightens, sight becomes, sound is heard, smell arouses, touch delights

---

[8] Rabbi Jonathan Sacks, 'Three Stages of Creation - Covenant & Conversation – Parshah' https://www.chabad.org/parshah/article_cdo/aid/4158654/jewish/Three-Stages-of-Creation.htm

and beauty colours. That the world is formed because something is always better than nothing. With this intention, God creates. The intention matters and our creativity is born from our hopes and dreams.

> The story of the cosmos and the story of humankind are a single story. The evolutionary history of the cosmos involves not only the movement from matter to life, and the movement from life to self-consciousness, but also the experience by conscious and free persons of God's self-communication by grace. If human beings are the cosmos come to consciousness before the grace of God, if they are the self-transcendence of matter, they remain profoundly interconnected with birds, rain forests, insects, photosynthesis, quantum particles and the Milky Way.[9]

And yet despite the grandeur of God's words, in our study of Scripture, the creation story translation has changed from, for example, 'a fourth day' to 'the fourth day' leading readers to a more literal interpretation of a seven day creation sequence. Yet time and days are not the important theme, for the Hebrew uses a cardinal number, one, in verse 5, so it actually reads 'one day' rather than 'the first day'. In our reading of the Creation myths, we are called to appreciate the bigger picture.

---

[9] Denis Edwards, *Jesus and the Cosmos*, (Eugene, OR: Wipf and Stock, 2004), 43.

> But do not ignore this one fact, beloved, that with the Lord one day is like a thousand years, and a thousand years are like one day.
>
> 2 Peter 3:8

Jewish days are calculated from sunset to sunset, following Genesis 1:5b, but in Genesis 1:5a, the light is presented first, so a day is initially presented as sunrise to sunrise. The point is that creation began with the creation of light. So, it is time for us to wake up and take note of what life has to offer.

The fact that God creates light in day one but not the sun, moon and stars until day four highlights the magnitude of God's power over other deities who cannot create light. Then following each of the first six days, we hear the refrain, 'there was evening and there was morning' (Genesis 1:5, 8, 13, 19, 23, 31). Each day begins in darkness and ends in the dawning of a new facet of creation.

> The power of God is pre-eminently the power to let things be. 'Let there be light' – the creative power is just the power that, because it results in things being what they are, in persons being who they are, cannot interfere with creatures. Obviously creating does not make any difference to things, it lets them be themselves. Creation is simply and solely letting things be, and our love is a faint image of that.[10]

God creates light first and so it is with our lives. We can only create in the light. The darkness is time for deep, silent

---

[10] Herbert McCabe, *God Matters*, (London: Geoffrey Chapman, 1987), 108.

sleep, but the light is our time to come alive, to create, to be. Light is our source of promise and hope.

> The Lord is my light and my salvation;
> whom shall I fear?
>
> Psalm 27:1

To allow what we have done in the day 'to be' and to allow ourselves in the evening 'to be'. A time of sleep, oblivious to the goings on in the world, a time to rest and so be awakened to a new enthusiasm for life, of immersing ourselves again in the daily dramas.

What is said, or done, or thought over, before our repose, and what enters our mind on awakening, says much about our head and heart space. Work seems to follow us to our beds and problems seem to stare us in the face when we awake. It is hard to shake them off. But there is the possibility to rest from these. The Christian practice of examination of conscience allows us to enter the night reconciled with ourselves and God.

- Set aside some quiet time for reflection
- Place yourself in God's presence
- Review the day
- Identify the positives and the negatives
- Seek forgiveness
- Set a goal for tomorrow
- Offer thanksgiving

By acknowledging the good, just as 'God saw it was good,' and noticing what could be better, we equip ourselves with satisfaction for a day's work and enthusiasm for the day ahead. Only then can we rest soundly at night. Appreciation, enthusiasm and anticipation determine our ability to rest and the drive to get up in the morning to face the light once again.

In creating day after day, we come to the awareness that a feature of the creation narrative in Genesis 1 is the separation of opposites into corresponding pairs. The first day is the separation of darkness from light, and the second day is the separation of the heavens above from the earth below (1:3-8).

> **Genesis 1:6-8** *And God said, 'Let there be a dome in the midst of the waters, and let it separate the waters from the waters'.* [7] *So God made the dome and separated the waters that were under the dome from the waters that were above the dome. And it was so.* [8] *God called the dome Sky. And there was evening and there was morning, the second day.*

The ancient world understanding of the structure of the universe as found in Genesis 1:6-9 regarded the earth as flat with mountains at the edges. Above it was a bowl-shaped sky or firmament, which separated the waters above from the waters below, and sealed off the edge of the earth from the waters surrounding everything. Stars were fixed to the dome of heaven, as were the sun called the 'greater light' and the moon, 'little light'. These moved around the sky. Rain came through floodgates in the firmament. Rivers, springs and seas came from the water under the earth by pushing up through the surface. Keeping the earth steady were pillars that supported it in the waters. These waters under the earth were the abode of the dead, or *Sheol*.

Of course, today we understand that there is no such dome. We have a sky that opens out into an ever-expanding universe. One of many universes! Planets, moons, stars, asteroids, black holes and galaxies. The God of ever-expanding imagination, of time travel. Our minds are to explore the magnanimity of all that is. The entire universe lies beyond, to be marvelled, as Saint Francis of Assisi did in his *Canticle of the Sun*:

> Praised be you, my Lord, with all your creatures, especially Brother Sun, who is the day and through whom you give us light. And he is beautiful and radiant with great splendour; and bears a likeness of you, Most High One.
>
> Praised be you, my Lord, through Sister Moon and the stars, in heaven you formed them clear and precious and beautiful.
>
> Praised be you, my Lord, through Brother Wind, and through the air, cloudy and serene, and every kind of weather through which you give substance to your creatures.
>
> Praised be you, my Lord, through Sister Water, which is very useful and humble and precious and chaste.
>
> Praised be you, my Lord, through Brother Fire, through whom you light the night and he is beautiful and playful and robust and strong.
>
> Praised be you, my Lord, through our Sister Mother Earth, who sustains and governs us, and who produces varied fruits with coloured flowers and herbs...

The sky is formed in the second day. A sky of evening and a sky of morning. Sunset and sunrise. Star studded and sun beamed. Moonstruck and cloud swept. The sky where heaven is hidden, where dreams cloud the imagination, where the wind plays with our fantasies, where the endless possibilities tease us. The sky is God's cover over us, a spectacular cover, where we are kept under God's care.

Why do we look at the sky, raise our minds and hearts upward? It is because it hides nothing from us. An interactive display board of ever-changing scenes and moods. And yet it also seems to hide so much more, beyond its vast stretches of boundless blue. In the Tower of Babel, to reach the heights became human's ambition.

> Come, let us build ourselves a city, and a tower with its top in the heavens.
>
> Genesis 11:1-9

The sky was where the rainbow of God's covenant was made with Noah.

> God said, 'This is the sign of the covenant that I make between me and you and every living creature that is with you, for all future generations: I have set my bow in the clouds, and it shall be a sign of the covenant between me and the earth. When I bring clouds over the earth and the bow is seen in the clouds'.
>
> Genesis 9:12-14

Over the centuries, the need to soar through the skies led to the invention of the aeroplane and flights to outer space.

Like the sky, there is no limit to human flights of fantasy. We are urged in the biblical narrative to look upon creation with wonder and awe. To see the endless horizons beckoning us, and yet to note the delicate intricacies of even the smallest of particles.

> To see a World in a Grain of Sand
> And a Heaven in a Wild Flower
> Hold Infinity in the palm of your hand
> And Eternity in an hour
>
> William Blake, 'Auguries of Innocence', 1863.

So, our journey has begun. We have been awakened to life. We are invited to travel on, explore and discover the wonderful world, the great expanse out there, and the minute details that surround us and in all this we will find our place.

Chapter 2

There is a wonderful world

Genesis 1:9-25

^{9}And God said, 'Let the waters under the sky be gathered together into one place, and let the dry land appear.' And it was so. ^{10}God called the dry land Earth, and the waters that were gathered together he called Seas. And God saw that it was good. ^{11}Then God said, 'Let the earth put forth vegetation: plants yielding seed, and fruit trees of every kind on earth that bear fruit with the seed in it.' And it was so. ^{12}The earth brought forth vegetation: plants yielding seed of every kind, and trees of every kind bearing fruit with the seed in it. And God saw that it was good. ^{13}And there was evening and there was morning, the third day.

^{14}And God said, 'Let there be lights in the dome of the sky to separate the day from the night; and let them be for signs and for seasons and for days and years, ^{15}and let them be lights in the dome of the sky to give light upon the earth.' And it was so. ^{16}God made the two great lights – the greater light to rule the day and the lesser light to rule the night – and the stars. ^{17}God set them in the dome of the sky to give light upon the earth, ^{18}to rule over the day and over the night, and to separate the light from the darkness. And God saw that it was good. ^{19}And there was evening and there was morning, the fourth day.

^{20}*And God said, 'Let the waters bring forth swarms of living creatures, and let birds fly above the earth across the dome of the sky.'* ^{21}*So God created the great sea monsters and every living creature that moves, of every kind, with which the waters swarm, and every winged bird of every kind. And God saw that it was good.* ^{22}*God blessed them, saying, 'Be fruitful and multiply and fill the waters in the seas, and let birds multiply on the earth.'* ^{23}*And there was evening and there was morning, the fifth day.*

^{24}*And God said, 'Let the earth bring forth living creatures of every kind: cattle and creeping things and wild animals of the earth of every kind.' And it was so.* ^{25}*God made the wild animals of the earth of every kind, and the cattle of every kind, and everything that creeps upon the ground of every kind. And God saw that it was good.*

Every day begins with God speaking. 'And God said' (1:9, 11, 24 and 26) and the approval formula, 'God saw' (1:10, 12, 25 and 31). All the initiative in creating lies with God.

^{9}*And God said, 'Let the waters under the sky be gathered together into one place, and let the dry land appear.' And it was so.*

^{10}*God called the dry land Earth, and the waters that were gathered together he called Seas. And God saw that it was good.*

^{11}*Then God said, 'Let the earth put forth vegetation: plants yielding seed, and fruit trees of every kind on earth that bear fruit with the seed in it.' And it was so.*

^{12}*The earth brought forth vegetation: plants yielding seed of every kind, and trees of every kind bearing fruit with the seed in it. And God saw that it was good.*

^{24}*And God said, 'Let the earth bring forth living creatures of every kind: cattle and creeping things and wild animals of the earth of every kind.' And it was so.* ^{25}*God made the wild animals of the earth of every kind, and the cattle of every kind, and everything that creeps upon the ground of every kind. And God saw that it was good.*

^{26}*Then God said, 'Let us make humankind in our image, according to our likeness; and let them have dominion over the fish of the sea, and over the birds of the air, and over the cattle, and over all the wild animals of the earth, and over every creeping thing that creeps upon the earth.'*

^{31}*God saw everything that he had made, and indeed, it was very good. And there was evening and there was morning, the sixth day.*

God creates the dry land earth and the seas, expansive landscapes, enduring, powerful, formidable, lasting beyond anyone's lifetime. We can spend our lives exploring them at great peril to ourselves. God has not created simply, hurriedly, distractedly. The earth's surface, sea and land, are strong, powerful, offering life but also death, beauty but also treachery, generosity but also severity, calmness but also wildness. And what a gift we have! A place to settle on and a place to escape to. A place that both blesses and challenges.

Genesis 1:9-10 *And God said, 'Let the waters under the sky be gathered together into one place, and let the dry land appear.' And it was so.* ^{10}*God called the dry land Earth, and the waters that were gathered together he called Seas. And God saw that it was good.*

The seas have created our love affair with water – fishing, sailing, swimming, diving, surfing. Water is understood as both life-giving but also destructive. The oceans and the seas, the rivers and creeks, the beaches and lagoons, the lakes and ponds. Bodies of water that provide a place for sea creatures and our own pleasure.

Aboriginals call the land their 'Mother'. It provides and cares for them. It is the land and sea that offers them food, water and shelter. It is the land that was created by Ancestral Beings and where they dwell in sacred sites. The biblical understanding was also that the land belonged not to humans but to God.

> The land shall not be sold in perpetuity, for the land is mine; with me you are but aliens and tenants.
> Leviticus 25:23

The gift of land to humans is not to be based on inheritance, settlement, conquest or international agreement. The gift of land follows from the generous word of God. A land we are blessed to be in.

Jesus turned to the natural world as a source of reflection and inspiration. Each prayer landscape provided a healing balm as Leonard Sweet and Frank Viola elaborate.

- Mountains and God-awareness: places of joy, revelation, awe and ecstasy.
- Deserts and self-awareness: places of spiritual discipline, introspection, inner struggle and insight.

- Water and others-awareness: places of relationship, power, peace, connection, trust and nourishment.
- Gardens and creation-awareness: places of wholeness, the presence of God, fulfilment, awareness, hope, growth and thriving.

The appeals of summit, wilderness, seascape, and garden were almost irresistible to Jesus' life. It is no accident that Jesus taught evangelism in the form of fishing lessons; and faith in the form of sleeping in a storm.[11] Much of what we need to know is experienced through our interaction with the natural surroundings.

The universe unfolds in God, who fills it completely. Hence, there is a mystical meaning to be found in a leaf, in a mountain trail, in a dewdrop, in a poor person's face. The ideal is not only to pass from the exterior to the interior to discover the action of God in the soul, but also to discover God in all things.

Pope Francis[12]

The mountains, deserts, waters and gardens. The landscapes that shape our hearts and minds. What they reveal to us is for the soothing of our souls.

---

[11] Leonard Sweet and Frank Viola, *Jesus. A Theography*, (Nashville: Thomas Nelson, 2012), 210-211, 214.

[12] Pope Francis, Encyclical on Climate change 2015 *Laudato Si'* (Praise be to you my Lord), paragraph 233. http://m.vatican.va/content/francescomobile/en/encyclicals/documents/papa-francesco_20150524_enciclica-laudato-si.html

Genesis 1:11-13 *Then God said, 'Let the earth put forth vegetation: plants yielding seed, and fruit trees of every kind on earth that bear fruit with the seed in it.' And it was so.* [12]*The earth brought forth vegetation: plants yielding seed of every kind, and trees of every kind bearing fruit with the seed in it. And God saw that it was good.* [13]*And there was evening and there was morning, the third day.*

This garden planet is miraculously created so that the waste product of trees, the oxygen, is the life-breath of humans, and the waste product of humans, carbon dioxide, is the life-breath of trees.

> I think that I shall never see
> A poem lovely as a tree.
> A tree whose hungry mouth is prest
> Against the earth's sweet flowing breast;
> A tree that looks at God all day,
> And lifts her leafy arms to pray;
> A tree that may in summer wear
> A nest of robins in her hair;
> Upon whose bosom snow has lain;
> Who intimately lives with rain.
> Poems are made by fools like me,
> But only God can make a tree.
> 'Trees' by Joyce Kilmer

Vegetation, our food supply, natural resources given for our sustenance. Herbs to add taste to our meals, plants rich in fibre for our digestion, greens for a healthy salad low on carbs, vegetables baked crisp and fruits of sweet delight. The deliciously wonderful variety of plant products to tease and sensationalise our taste buds while providing the nourishment our body requires. We are indeed living in a rich world that is to our benefit.

> [13] Blessed by the LORD be his land, with the choice gifts of heaven above, and of the deep that lies beneath; [14] with the choice fruits of the sun, and the rich yield of the months; [15] with the finest produce of the ancient mountains, and the abundance of the everlasting hills; [16] with the choice gifts of the earth and its fullness, and the favour of the one who dwells on Sinai.
>
> Deuteronomy 33:13-16

God's planet is filled with abundance for our nourishment and yet many starve. We take the natural resources of seeds and fruits and have made a global market out of what should be freely provided. The natural resources are not to be hoarded and profiteered from. The seeds and plants of the earth are for everyone's benefit.

> Then he told them a parable: 'The land of a rich man produced abundantly. [17] And he thought to himself, "What should I do, for I have no place to store my crops?" [18] Then he said, "I will do this: I will pull down my barns and build larger ones, and there I will store all my grain and my goods. [19] And I will say to my soul, Soul, you have ample goods laid up for many years; relax, eat, drink, be merry." [20] But God said to him, "You fool! This very night your life is being demanded of you. And the things you have prepared, whose will they be?" [21] So it is with those who store up treasures for themselves but are not rich towards God'.
>
> Luke 12:16-21

Happy are those who know how to cultivate the seed from their garden yield and thus live sustainably. God encourages our own efforts at sustenance, not peddling for a global market that goes so far as to patent seeds and produce seedless fruits so as to have a stranglehold on the fruits of the earth.

The world is our dining table! Organic foods was God's first gift. A generous world of greens. To eat of the plants given and to use their products for healing and soothing. We have vegetables, fruits, herbs, nuts, spices, seasoning, juices, oils... and the list goes on.

Yet we take for granted the food on our table. We want ready-made dishes and have lost an appreciation for the land. We are too detached from the sweat and tears, the furrowing and watering, the sowing and waiting, the sprouting and budding, the blossoming and harvesting, the cropping and plucking, the threshing and storing. We need to take ourselves out into the open wide world, into our backyards, to countrysides, to rural communities, and to learn once more the value of land.

And as we get off our lounges, out of our Covid lockdown and out of imposed restrictions, maybe once again we can appreciate the world. To journey is to go beyond our limited confines. To stretch the mind and the legs. To appreciate awakening and sleeping, travelling and resting. And God already knew that.

Genesis 1:14-19 *And God said, 'Let there be lights in the dome of the sky to separate the day from the night; and let them be for signs and for seasons and for days and years, ^{15}and let them be lights in the dome of the sky to give light* *upon the earth.' And it was so.* ¹⁶*God made the two great lights – the greater light to rule the day and the lesser light to rule the night – and the stars.* ¹⁷*God set them in the dome of the sky to give light upon the earth,* ¹⁸*to rule over the day and over the night, and to separate the light from the darkness. And God saw that it was good.* ¹⁹*And there was evening and there was morning, the fourth day.*

The first Genesis creation account ends off each phase of creating with, 'there was evening and there was morning'. We may contemplate the night sky but we wait for the morning sun to begin our lives again. So what is the purpose of the creation of light?

- It separates day from night
- Separates light from darkness
- It determines the seasons, days and years
- Gives light
- Rules the day
- Rules the night

God created light first and kept it going even in the night, for one cannot live without light. The stars and moon offer guidance when all appears dark. It is a comforting act. God will not lose us to darkness! A twenty-four hour availability of God. There is never a moment of life without light and hope. In separating 'light from the darkness', nothing is meant to overwhelm or quench the light.

God is light and in him there is no darkness at all.

1 John 1:5

> As long as I am in the world, I am the light of the world.
>
> John 9:5

> Be the light of the world.
>
> Matthew 5:14

Why the persistent insistence on light? Because of our human inclination at times to hide in the night, to be consumed by the dark and be overwhelmed. Yet God will not abandon us to darkness of mind, heart and soul.

It is better if we can be in the warmth of the sun and to see in the light of day. Light rests lightly on our minds whereas darkness is a heavy blanket upon us. Light lifts us up. It makes us feel light as a feather. To lighten up the face. To light up a room. To lighten the load. To be enlightened.

The day and sunlight. We need a summertime of open doors, streaming light, lazy days in the sun. A time to pause and relish life, to know we are loved, to take pleasure in what we are, to awaken to ourselves and God's working in us. Shadows are gone, fear has dissipated, and darkness is far removed. In summer, it is time to shine and be warmed with hopes, dreams and aspirations.

But summers are not meant to last and Autumn steps in with a cool change and at times it is a welcome guest from the oppressive heat. Autumn is a time to recognise that life is passing and all things change. It eases us into a new pattern of knowing and being. There is a need to let go of what hinders us. Just as the tree sheds its leaves when the time comes, we too need to shed our old habits and let go.

In Winter, we experience a time of slowing down, cuddling up and resting through the longer cold nights. In the winter of our lives, there are lessons waiting to be learnt, hope wanting to glimmer.

Then comes Spring, a time to prepare for those occasions of new blooming and growth. A time to reawaken to life again and enjoy the world around us.

Welcome to the ongoing journey called life. And there was evening and there was morning.

And as with the days and nights, seasons and times, we become more and more immersed in life. On our life's journey, we become ever more aware of what is around us, the manifold manifestations of life.

> **Genesis 1:20-23** *And God said, 'Let the waters bring forth swarms of living creatures, and let birds fly above the earth across the dome of the sky.'* [21] *So God created the great sea monsters and every living creature that moves, of every kind, with which the waters swarm, and every winged bird of every kind. And God saw that it was good.* [22] *God blessed them, saying, 'Be fruitful and multiply and fill the waters in the seas, and let birds multiply on the earth.'* [23] *And there was evening and there was morning, the fifth day.*

Ah, that desire to soar high as a bird, to fly, fly, fly away. If only we could learn from the birds to allow our minds to soar, to enjoy the freedom, take in the wide scenic view, to allow the wind to caress our faces and tumble our hair as we glide through life with ease.

Or to swim across vast oceans like the darting of fish, or the agile dolphins among the waves. If only we could learn to dive in the deep, to plunge ourselves into cold, dark waters and explore our depths. To immerse ourselves in waters of wonder.

Or to run at full speed over vast stretches of land, our feet barely touching the ground. What wonderful creatures that we envy with their prowess, skills and abilities. We humans can feel so heavy, slow, cumbersome. Yet creatures of life can coax us into living courageously.

> All things counter, original, spare, strange;
> Whatever is fickle, freckled (who knows how?)
> With swift, slow; sweet, sour; adazzle, dim;
> He fathers-forth whose beauty is past change:
> Praise him.

'Pied Beauty' by Gerard Manley Hopkins (1844-1889)

In taking a closer look at the creation of sea life and birds in the first chapter of Genesis, we note:

- Swarms of living creatures
- Fly above the earth
- Great sea monsters
- Every living creature
- Every kind, with which the waters swarm
- Every winged bird of every kind
- Be fruitful
- Multiply
- Fill the waters in the seas
- Let birds multiply on the earth

It is a frenzy of creation, an abundance of life, a flurry of happenings, alive, abuzz, a cacophony of excitement, with hustling and bustling. God creates a world fully alive. Life continually begets new life, there is movement and competition, colour and beauty, flocks of birds, schools of fish, loving the freedom to be.

And then we read the command to 'be fruitful and multiply'. To be fruitful, to contribute positively and generously to each day, and to allow things to happen.

> It is the adventure of emerging life transcending limitations and attaining a richer flourishing, of creation's potent capacity for novelty and the transcendence of limitation.
>
> Timothy Radcliffe[13]

'To multiply' is to propagate one's species. To increase the number of sea creatures, birds or humans. Yet God does not command this of the 'animals of the earth' (1:24). Why the omission? Perhaps because on land, survival is much more difficult with human presence. The seas and the skies are more out of reach or less accessible to the interference of humankind and so sea creatures and birds can flourish in number. Yet is that so? We have conquered the sea to the point where there is critical shortage of marine life. We shoot birds as a pastime! The propagation of species and the command to multiply is not as easy as called for. Species extinction is on the rise. Yes, God was right in saying multiply! Bring forth new life. Bring to birth creatures so

---

[13] Timothy :Radcliffe, *Alive in God. A Christian Imagination*, (London: Bloomsbury Continuum, 2019), 58.

that the splendid variety of life will not disappear before our very eyes.

> To lessen the grandeur of the outer world is to limit the fulfilment available to our inner world. For the stars in the night sky over our cities to be blocked from view by particle and light pollution is not simply the loss of a passing visual experience, it is a loss of soul. This is especially a loss for children, for it is from the stars, the planets, and the moon in the heavens as well as from the flowers, birds, forests, and woodland creatures of Earth that some of their most profound inner experiences originate. To devastate any aspect of the natural world is to distort the sublime experiences that provide fulfilment to the human mode of being.
>
> Thomas Berry[14]

The world was created to be inhabited, to be explored, to be a home – the waters swarm with life, the skies welcome birds of flight, and animals roam the earth. Life necessitates the continual begetting of life so that the world continues to have splendour and colour, sound and soul. The world is meant to be teeming with life, a world of celebrations, of company, of comings and goings, all in open display.

> To wantonly destroy a living species is to silence forever a divine voice.
>
> Thomas Berry[15]

---

[14] Thomas Berry, *The Sacred Universe. Earth, Spirituality, and Religion in the Twenty-First Century*, edited by Mary Evelyn Tucker, (New York: Columbia University Press, 2009), 132.
[15] Thomas Berry, *The Dream of the Earth*, (Berkeley: Counterpoint, 2015).

Without human interference, the sea creatures and birds would spawn much spectacular life. God gives us diversions of beauty to capture our minds.

In the Catholic tradition, there are two spiritual pathways – the *kataphatic* and the *apophatic*. The *kataphatic* tradition (way of affirmation) emphasises beauty that is revealed and apparent. It uses words, images, symbols, ideas. The *apophatic* tradition (way of negation) dwells on glory that remains concealed and hidden from view. It is the practice to empty the mind and simply rest in the presence of God. We need both traditions *kataphatic* and *apophatic*, to better know God.

Glorious abundance, breathtaking wonder, showcase of extravagance, symphony of sights and sounds. And yet like a solitary bird, silently soaring sky high. There is God in the throbbing and living out of life. And there is God in the quiet solitary moments of a resting creation.

Be fruitful and multiply – energy, propagation, lovemaking, procreating, social ongoings, gatherings, life-giving. And yet 'there was evening' a time to slow down, quiet, solitude and rest. Then 'there was morning' to be awake once again, encounters, conversations and play. And once again, a world of rest, quiet, alone time and slumber. And the cycle goes on – *kataphatic* moments and *apophatic* moments. And God is there all along, in this life of song and dance, of mystery and awe.

In this journey of creation, enough is not enough. Continuing creativity and continual becoming is part of the journey.

> **Genesis 1:24-25** *And God said, 'Let the earth bring forth living creatures of every kind: cattle and creeping things and wild animals of the earth of every kind.' And it was so.* ^{25}*God made the wild animals of the earth of every kind, and the cattle of every kind, and everything that creeps upon the ground of every kind. And God saw that it was good.*

Animism is the belief that natural objects, natural phenomena, and the universe itself possess souls. Pantheism is the view that God is identical with the cosmos. Yet the author of Genesis chapter one makes it clear that God is distinct from creation; and creation is not equal to the divine. Even so, God creates what is important, necessary and beautiful for our becoming. Aboriginals well understood this deep connection with the earth.

> The land is my mother. Like a human mother, the land gives us protection, enjoyment and provides our needs – economic, social and religious. We have a human relationship with the land: mother, daughter, son. When the land is taken from us or destroyed, we feel hurt because we belong to the land and we are part of it.
>
> Djinyini Gondarra

> Our spirituality is a oneness and an interconnectedness with all that lives and breathes, even with all that does not live or breathe.
>
> Mudrooroo

The first creation story (Genesis 1:1 to 2:4a) dedicates three verses and an entire day to the creation of birds and all the creatures of the oceans (1:20–22). Humans share the sixth day with other land animals and the literary structure weaves their creation together. To live is to be united with the life around us.

In the biblical account, creation happens developmentally over six days, and a pairing of things. Nothing exists on its own, simply just for itself.

Day 1: The light (1:4)

Day 2: The earth and the seas (1:10)

Day 3: Vegetation of all kind (1:12)

Day 4: The lights, both sun and stars (1:18)

Day 5: Sea creatures and birds (1:21)

Day 6: Animals and land creatures (1:25)

From the very first moment when God said, 'Let there be light' (1:3), it was the first of many illuminating moments. It was a good thing. And so followed rapid succession, one created thing after another. Life begets life. Beauty begets beauty. From light immediately follows the creation of the sky, the formation of earth and seas, plants and vegetation, sun and moon and stars, followed by marine life, bird life and then land creatures, and finally humans.

Yet God does not create alone but engages other parts of creation:

- In 1:11 God said let the earth put forth vegetation and the earth does so
- In 1:16 the sun and moon rule day and night
- In 1:20 God said let the waters bring forth living creatures and birds

- In 1:24 God said let the earth bring forth living creatures
- In 1:26-28 humans rule on God's behalf

God creates wonderful things but what is created cannot take care of itself. Ongoing attention is required. Life is not a sequenced, mechanical evolution. It is a complex process, it develops and changes. Each element of creation is influenced by its surroundings and in turn shapes it.

> It is characteristic of God to create in an emergent and evolutionary way.
>
> Denis Edwards[16]

So, is it the earth that brings forth, or is it God that makes? It is the ongoing argument of how did things come to be. We can trace an evolutionary history and explain that life emerged and begat more complex life. Yet how did it all begin? We therefore argue that God is in the picture too. The waters and earth cannot simply create creatures. God creates new forms of life out of nothing. It takes that spark of the divine to help us create newness of life. On our own, we can do nothing.

Creation is a splendid expression of all that is, dependency and yet independent, together as a whole yet individually unique. As Paul understood it, all things in the world come together under Christ.

---

[16] Denis Edwards, *Ecology at the Heart of Faith*, (Maryknoll, New York: Orbis Books, 2006), 11.

> As a plan for the fullness of time, to gather up all things in him, things in heaven and things on earth.
>
> Ephesians 1:10
> (see also Romans 8:21-22; Colossians 1:20)

Cattle and creeping things and wild animals – the domesticated, the farm animals, the wild ones, the creepy and crawly. Animals we have tamed, animals we use for their products, animals we fear. The world is home to every sort of creature imaginable. All of God's creatures make up the 'kin-dom' of God and we all tread the same 'holy ground'.

We cannot expect uniformity and similarity. Life is to expect diversity and differences. If that is the case with animals, so extend that understanding to the diversity of humans. Humans are not able to domesticate or tame all creatures. The wild is there to be free and uninhibited, to roam and hunt. The cattle and other animals suffice for our human needs. Each has its own way.

> The spiritual life cannot be made suburban. It is always frontier, and we who live in it must accept and even rejoice that it remains untamed.
>
> Howard Macey

To realise that differences all play a rich symphony of creative energy. All things are connected, united, reflected, patterned in the life of God. Cattle and creeping things and wild animals, God saw all this as very good. All things speak to us of God. The ever-present God in all forms, shapes, sizes and colours. We are to live on this planet in harmony, as the Prophet Isaiah notes:

⁶The wolf shall live with the lamb,
   the leopard shall lie down with the kid,
the calf and the lion and the fatling together,
   and a little child shall lead them.
⁷The cow and the bear shall graze,
   their young shall lie down together;
   and the lion shall eat straw like the ox.
⁸The nursing child shall play over the hole of the asp,
   and the weaned child shall put its hand on the adder's den.
⁹They will not hurt or destroy
   on all my holy mountain;
for the earth will be full of the knowledge of the LORD
   as the waters cover the sea.

Isaiah 11:6-9

So as we settle into this wonderful world, it is time we humans began to better understand our place and purpose here.

Chapter 3

With people

Genesis 1:26-30

^{26}Then God said, 'Let us make humankind in our image, according to our likeness; and let them have dominion over the fish of the sea, and over the birds of the air, and over the cattle, and over all the wild animals of the earth, and over every creeping thing that creeps upon the earth.'

^{27}So God created humankind in his image,
in the image of God he created them;
male and female he created them.

^{28}God blessed them, and God said to them, 'Be fruitful and multiply, and fill the earth and subdue it; and have dominion over the fish of the sea and over the birds of the air and over every living thing that moves upon the earth.' ^{29}God said, 'See, I have given you every plant yielding seed that is upon the face of all the earth, and every tree with seed in its fruit; you shall have them for food. ^{30}And to every beast of the earth, and to every bird of the air, and to everything that creeps on the earth, everything that has the breath of life, I have given every green plant for food.' And it was so.

God speaks in the third person when God creates the plants and the animals, but in the case of the human being, God speaks in the first person (Genesis 1:26), and so ordains the uniqueness of humankind as a species.

> Let *us* make humankind
> in *our* image
> according to *our* likeness

Unlike the other creatures, human beings do not have their own point of reference in themselves but in God.

> God created humankind (*ha'adam*) in his image,
> in the image of God he created him (*'oto*);
> male and female he created them (*'otam*).

Barbara Reid explains this verse in depth:

- The first line speaks of humankind as one creature, ha'adam, which means literally, 'earth creature' (the Hebrew word for earth is *adama*).
- Line two repeats that humanity, regarded as one creature, is created in the image of God. The pronoun is singular, *'oto*, 'him,' translated as a plural 'them' in the NRSV, rightly capturing that the pronoun has 'a collective, common gender sense'.
- The final line clarifies the idea that, although humankind is one, it comprises both male and female (now the pronoun is plural, *'otam*, 'them'), created thus by God.[17]

---

[17] Barbara E. Reid, *Wisdom's Feast. An Invitation to Feminist Interpretation of the Scriptures*, (Grand Rapids, Michigan: William B. Eerdmans Publishing Company, 2016), 16-17.

Genesis 1:27 affirms that male and female together are created in the divine image. Given that, in other ancient Near Eastern religions, statues or images of the god were thought to make the god present to worshippers, we have here God with us, and we are like God.

> ... Yet still an absence
> Disturbed me. I slept and dreamed
> Of a likeness, fashioning it,
> When I woke, to a slow
> Music; in love with it
> For itself, giving it freedom
> To love me, risking the disappointment.
>
> 'Making' by R. S. Thomas

If by 'image' it is meant that human beings have something in their nature which is like God, then the question arises: Is it a physical correspondence or a spiritual likeness? According to William J. Dumbrell, image refers not to visible likeness but to the mental and spiritual qualities that humans share with their Creator.[18] The fundamental meaning of the phrase 'image of God' is that God has created creatures able to be in interpersonal relationship with God. Humankind is created so that something can happen between God and the human community. Karl Barth sees it as 'a Thou which can be addressed by God and an I which is responsible before God'. We thus have a call and responsibility in and for our lives.

---

[18] William J. Dumbrell, *Covenant and Creation. An Old Testament Covenant Theology*, (Milton Keynes: Paternoster, 2013), 30.

... Selves — goes itself; *myself* it speaks and spells,
Crying Whát I dó is me: for that I came.

I say móre: the just man justices;
Keeps grace: thát keeps all his goings graces;
Acts in God's eye what in God's eye he is —
Chríst — for Christ plays in ten thousand places,
Lovely in limbs, and lovely in eyes not his
To the Father through the features of men's faces.

>   Gerard Manley Hopkins, *As Kingfishers Catch Fire*

We are in the image and likeness of God. Teilhard de Chardin postulates God as the goal toward which all things are moving. The cosmic story has a direction, an 'Omega Point'. The universe has made 'progress' toward higher degrees of complexity: pre-atomic, atomic, molecular, unicellular, multi-cellular, vertebrate, primate and human stages of increasing complexity over billions of years. Matter has attained a higher degree of complexity and the universe has exploded into 'thought' through humans. The cosmic impulse to maximise complexity and consciousness is still going on, even in the face of forces such as destruction, despair, evil and death. The earth is becoming more complex, clothing itself in something analogous to a brain as a result of developments in technology, education, economics, global politics and the internet. Teilhard refers to this emergent phenomenon as the 'noosphere'. Our own destiny is inseparable from the universe that has given birth to us, explains John F.

Haught.[19] Continuing Pierre Teilhard de Chardin's thoughts, we read:

> evolution and Christianity coincide fundamentally. On the one hand, modern evolutionism has ceased to be materialist and determinist in orientation and by definition. As the most authoritative scientists admit (Haldane, Julian Huxley and so on), the universe, as now revealed to us by facts, is moving towards higher states of consciousness and spirituality – exactly as in the Christian *Weltanschauung*. And, on the other hand, Christianity, its sensibilities aroused by the conquests of modern thought, is finally becoming alive to the fact that its three fundamental personalist mysteries are in reality simply the three aspects of one and the same process (Christogenesis) considered either in its motive principal (creation), or its unifying mechanism (incarnation), or in its ascensional work (redemption); and so we find ourselves in the main stream of evolution.[20]

He continues on:

> Only to the Christian is it given to be able to locate at the summit of space-time not merely a vague, cold *something* but a warm and well-defined *someone*; and so *hic et nunc* only he in all the world is in a position to believe *utterly* in evolution – evolution that is no longer simply personalizing, but is personalized –

---

[19] John F. Haught, 'Teilhard de Chardin: Action, Contemplation, and the Cosmos' in *Radical Grace*, April-June 2010, Vol 23, nos 2, 5.

[20] Pierre Teilhard de Chardin, *Christianity and Evolution*, translated by Rene Hague, (London: A Harvest Book, 1969), 155.

and (what is psychologically even more important) to dedicate himself to it *with love*.[21]

That humans are evolution become conscious of itself was proposed by Julian Huxley, while Athanasius spoke of 'deification', John Calvin referred to 'sanctification', Karl Rahner applied the term 'divinisation' and Pierre Teilhard de Chardin coined the phrase 'convergent evolution' toward the Omega Point. James Carroll sums it up by stating humans are on the move toward God.[22]

In Ilia Delio's view, the direction of evolution is toward the maximisation of goodness, especially if the incarnation is the goal of evolution.[23] Or, as Brain Swimme writes:

> The deepening of the consciousness necessary to hear the story of the universe required the complexification of consciousness coming from all four million years of the human journey. The human is the space created in the universe process for hearing and celebrating the stories of the universe that fill the universe.[24]

Our coming into being, as conscious creation, was to come into a greater awareness and appreciation of all life. If, in our understanding, it is God that creates us, then it follows that we who are God's creation must somehow

---

[21] Pierre Teilhard de Chardin, *Christianity and Evolution*, p. 156.
[22] James Carroll, *Christ Actually. The Son of God for the Secular Age*, (London: William Collins, 2014), 274.
[23] Ilia Delio, *Christ in Evolution*, (Maryknoll, N.Y.: Orbis Books, 2013), 7.
[24] Brian Swimme, *The Hidden Heart of the Cosmos: Humanity and the New Story*, (Maryknoll: Orbis Books, 1996).

be connected not only to God but to the creation from which we were birthed. This is witnessed through being in connection with the Spirit, our living in the world as caretakers, through modifying our hunger in order to live sustainably, and by encouraging a communal mindset rather than continual indulgence in individualistic desires. Joan Chittister writes in *The Monastic Way* about humans being created in God's image

> Michelangelo's *Creation of Adam*, for instance, makes a bold theological statement: The bond between God and Adam in this great work of art was clearly not based on submission. God reaches out to Adam to call him to life and to deputize him to bring that life to fullness. Adam, in one great glance of God, becomes bearer of the life of God.
>
> ... The human being, strong and virile, is created to be partner with God in the human enterprise. The human being rises to continue the work of God. Michelangelo proclaims in full color and almost lifelike vigor that to be created is to be called to responsibility, to competency, to effectiveness.[25]

Insofar as we have existence, we exist because of God. We share in the being of the original, in the being of God. In the image of God, we can share all things with God. We are called to more fully live on earth in accordance to this pattern of deification. It is a movement from lesser to greater reality.

---

[25] Joan Chittister, *The Monastic Way*, http://joanchittister.org/word-from-joan/monastic-way-0

And yet, God has no image. 'I am who I am' also translated, 'I will be what I will be' says God to Moses in Exodus 3:13. 'Image' then must refer to something quite different than the possession of a specific form. The fundamental point of Genesis 1 is that God transcends nature, according to Rabbi Jonathan Sacks and therefore, God is free, unbounded by nature's laws. By creating human beings 'in his image', God gave us a similar freedom, thus creating one capable itself of being creative, of self-transcendence, immortal longings, the sole life-form capable of dialogue with the Author of life.[26]

We are called, as God's image, to imitate God, 'Be holy, for I, the LORD your God, am holy' (Leviticus 19:2).

If we are created in God's 'image', then each of us has value as we are. Nothing else can make us more important. Our wealth, intelligence, beauty, skills, titles, possessions, etc., do not add to our status. They all play second fiddle to the claim that we are first and foremost human in the image of the divine. That is who we are and our inspiration. Anything else is a diversion from our true selves. And that is why the greatest pursuit of humans is for God.

God creates humans bare, naked, just as they are. To identify one another according to nationality, creed, race, culture, sect, faith, skin colour, speech, dress, etc., is to diminish the greater person standing before us. The only distinction God gives to the human is sex, 'male and female'. Aside from this, God makes no other distinction.

---

[26] Rabbi Jonathan Sacks, *Covenant and Conversation: A weekly reading of the Jewish Bible. Genesis: The Book of Beginnings*, (New Milford, USA: Maggid Books, 2009), 21.

Yet the tendency to claim that all creatures have equal value and that there is no special place for the human undermines the biblical view of the uniqueness of the human made in the image of God, the struggle of social justice and ecological commitment. As Denis Edwards noted, human beings have a unique moral responsibility for other creatures to respond creatively and wisely.[27]

Just as human ingenuity has been used to plunder the natural world, so humans can use their God-given creativity and intelligence to bring about growth and healing to the earth and all living creatures.

The presence of humans on this planet matters. It matters so much that our actions can have both positive and negative implications. Whatever our choices and actions, our lives and the livelihood of the planet is in our hands, generation to generation.

> **Genesis 1:28** *God blessed them, and God said to them, 'Be fruitful and multiply, and fill the earth and subdue it; and have dominion over the fish of the sea and over the birds of the air and over every living thing that moves upon the earth.'*

In the first creation account, God creates step by step and lastly creates humankind. It is only in the creation of humans do we read, 'God blessed them'. God's blessing is a message of hope and promise. Blessing is needed for

---

[27] Denis Edwards, *Ecology at the heart of faith*, (Maryknoll, New York: Orbis Books, 2006), 22.

humans are poised between good and evil. We need divine grace to guide us in the ways of God.

> When I look at your heavens, the work of your fingers,
>   the moon and the stars that you have established;
> ⁴what are human beings that you are mindful of them,
>   mortals that you care for them?
> ⁵Yet you have made them a little lower than God,
>   and crowned them with glory and honour.
> ⁶You have given them dominion over the works of your hands;
>   you have put all things under their feet,
> ⁷all sheep and oxen,
>   and also the beasts of the field,
> ⁸the birds of the air, and the fish of the sea,
>   whatever passes along the paths of the seas.
>
> Psalm 8:3-8

'God blessed them, and God said... subdue it; and have dominion.' It means bringing the world under God's care. It is to rule over those who are not of the same kind and who may be viewed as potentially hostile. In setting humankind and the creatures in a shared world, God is providing for an order in which all living creatures may be sustained. Humans are tasked to produce a state in which the earth can support life through careful nurture of creation.

So do we view nature as alien and terrifying? Is it something we desire to dominate and subdue? Or, as Denis Edwards understands it, is the human vocation one of bringing human intelligence, courage, and work to bear on the land so that herds might flourish and crops might grow?[28]

In the biblical narrative, the one who most fully exercises divinely ordained 'dominion' is Noah, who preserves the diversity of all creation (Genesis 7:8-9).

For an ancient agrarian society, the command to dominate gave divine warrant to cultivate the land and harness its fertility for sustaining life, human and nonhuman.[29] The human task is therefore to:

- Be fruitful
- Multiply
- Fill the earth
- Subdue it
- Have dominion

Fill the earth and allow the earth to fill you. Explore, become one with the earth, travel, seek, search, study it, know it, populate it, treasure it, love it. A world to be lived in and enjoyed, generation after generation. A world that you are invited to feel a sense of belonging to and of responsibility for.

God creates each creature, sustains its existence, delights in its goodness, and blesses it with fertility. Human beings are a part of God's creation, interrelated with all other creatures yet called to act responsibly before God

---

[28] Edwards, *Ecology at the heart of faith*, 20.
[29] William P Brown, 'Biblical Accounts of Creation' in *The Old Testament and Ethics. A book-by-book survey*. Joel B. Green and Jacqueline E. Lapsley, Editors, (Grand Rapids, Michigan: Baker Academic, 2013), 166.

within creation. It offers a fundamentally God-centred (theocentric) vision of reality rather than a human-centered (anthropocentric) one.[30]

So God has created humans in God's image and likeness. God directs us to take responsibility for life on the planet and to ensure its ongoing order. God calls us to propagate our own species and provide that freedom to all other creatures. But that is not all. As we take care of creation, God takes care of us.

> **Genesis 1:29-30** *God said, 'See, I have given you every plant yielding seed that is upon the face of all the earth, and every tree with seed in its fruit; you shall have them for food.*
> *And to every beast of the earth, and to every bird of the air, and to everything that creeps on the earth, everything that has the breath of life, I have given every green plant for food.' And it was so.*

God not only creates but ensures the nourishment of all living things. For humans, every plant with seeds and trees with fruit is ours to eat. For everything that has the breath of life, green plants have been given to consume.

Sustenance is an inherent need of all life forms. God feeds us and feeds all living creatures. The two verses that describe the creation of terrestrial creatures (1:24–25) ends with provisions for their feeding (1:30). God's provision of food suggests that God values and cares for humans and

---

[30] Denis Edwards, *Ecology at the heart of faith*, (Maryknoll, New York: Orbis Books, 2006), 19.

for creatures. Note, however, humans are not given other animals as food. Our carnivorous side emerges later.

In providing food for our sustenance, we read that this food was located 'upon the face of all the earth'. It implies that all of creation, wherever we may be, is for our nourishment. No one should go hungry. 'You shall have them for food.' God's intent was that no one would go hungry. Malnutrition and starvation which plague our world oppose the purpose of creation. The duty and obligation of every person created in God's image is to offer hospitality, to feed and be fed. It is an act of generosity we are each called to – to share the bounteous riches of nature, an act of social justice. Everyone has a right to eat and be nourished.

This invitation to eat of the fruits of the earth is again reiterated in Genesis 2:16. The invitation to share a meal and the opportunity to enjoy, gather and be satisfied.

Food is a necessity, and the food chain is essential. One creature consumed by another, which in turn is consumed by another. And the cycle goes on. Creatures must multiply; in many cases, they must spawn hundreds of progeny for a few to survive to maturity. The Genesis account clearly puts the call 'Be fruitful and multiply' (1:22) prior to the invitation to eat (1:30). Living creatures depend on other living creatures for food. It is a process of be fruitful and multiply and consume and be consumed.

Food provided to nourish. To enable growth and hence the ability to multiply. To stave off starvation. To enjoy. To gather together at table. Food is our sustenance and life force.

In our hunger, we have widened our food sources, tasted other delights, savoured delicacies, cooked and baked, boiled and fried, salted and sweetened, preserved and canned our food supplies.

Yet the eating habits of humans has changed over time. From herbivores to carnivores to omnivores. Today, we have vegans, vegetarians, meat lovers, pescatarians and so on. Then there are those who have food allergies, who are lactose intolerant, glutton free, nut free, etc.

In all these ways and modes, consideration is to be given to eating in moderation, mindful of those who have little food to sustain them. To reap and gather, purchase and consume, only that which we need. Unfortunately, too often we become gluttons in our consuming. Let there be self-control which is the better practice. And allow enjoyment of company and value of nourishment to direct what and how we eat.

Chapter 4

Life is a blessing

The creation account in the first chapter of the Book of Genesis detailed step by step the coming into being of the sun, moon, stars, earth – with its natural features of flora and fauna – and of humanity.

The creative narrative was written over 2000 years ago when people were not privy to evolution theories, DNA tracing, fossil records, carbon dating, archaeological digs, etc. Today, science summarises the evolutionary history of the world as a series of five steps which, by and large, support the sequence of events outlined in the creation accounts.

- The beginning of the universe (the big bang)
- The evolution of stars and planets
- The origin of life
- The evolution of life
- The origin of humankind

So now in the journey it is time to celebrate the splendour of creation as God did.

Genesis 1:31 to 2:2 *God saw everything that he had made, and indeed, it was very good. And there was evening and there was morning, the sixth day.*
²Thus the heavens and the earth were finished, and all their multitude.

In the Book of Genesis, 'God saw all he had made, and indeed it was very good'. This sums up the inherent goodness of God's created world. Every living thing has intrinsic value. Creation has meaning and purpose including:

- All of creation and every creature is 'sacramental', embodying and expressing something of God
- Unification of the whole known cosmos
- The diversity of creatures symbolises the abundance of God, who enables creatures to be and to become
- Freedom and opportunity to develop of one's own accord

Chance, necessity, choice and relationships form the fundamental system by which freedom is bestowed on the cosmos by its Creator.

> The day of my awakening was the day I saw and knew I saw all things in God and God in all things.
> Mechtilde of Magdeburg (1207-1282)

'God saw everything.' God is about awareness, giving time and appreciation to what is. Stopping and seeing. To notice the hidden and the obvious. To see detail but also the larger picture. To be attentive to all. It takes time as we read, 'there was evening and there was morning'. Our days are to be spent in taking note of what is around us, acknowledging and recognising purpose and beauty. If we have ever really observed our everyday lives, we would have noticed all things coming together, that there is goodness, thoughtfulness, a deep peace and unity.

> Entranced by those great homogenous systems – ocean, air, desert – man, poised over emptiness and silence, locked up within himself, envies the intimate fusion of the drops of water in the seas, of the molecules in the atmosphere; and he glimpses the bliss there would be in becoming more intermingled with Another, in sinking deeper and deeper into it, like smoke that vanishes, like the sound that dies away in space, like the stone that slips gently down to the bottom of the sea.[31]

Day by day, God sees and notices creation. Day by day, we too are called to see more and more of life. To see is to be engaged with reality. To be open-eyed with wonder. To notice that, beyond the mundane and troublesome, there is much more going on. Despite appearances of bleakness, there is a larger world of possibilities. Life is not just about our small story but also the wider horizon, the larger vision that encompasses much more of life and hence greater hope. To understand that life is untamed and frightening but also beautiful and amazing. This is where we can find peace and fulfilment. Appreciation for this world waits and continues to wait.

---

[31] Teilhard de Chardin, 'Struggle Against the Multitude,' in *Writings in Time of War*, Translated René Hague, (New York: Harper and Row, 1968).

Just as God looked and saw it was good, we must learn to look and see goodness. Take one long sweeping look outdoors, outback, away from the urban sprawl. Indeed, it is very good. Creation is magnificent, glorious, inspiring, wonderful. It is very good! But...

We have created houses and fences and virtual reality and have forgotten there is a world to explore! The entire world is at our doorstep and we choose to close the door and remain inside. Wake up. See. Look. Take in. Appreciate. Enjoy everything. God is generous, giving us a world of wonder to delight in.

> ³Praise him, sun and moon;
>   praise him, all you shining stars!
> ⁴Praise him, you highest heavens,
>   and you waters above the heavens!
> ⁷Praise the LORD from the earth,
>   you sea monsters and all deeps,
> ⁸fire and hail, snow and frost,
>   stormy wind fulfilling his command!
> ⁹Mountains and all hills,
>   fruit trees and all cedars!
> ¹⁰Wild animals and all cattle,
>   creeping things and flying birds!
>
> Psalm 148:3-4, 7-10

And God saw that it was good (Genesis 1:4, 10, 12, 18, 21, 25) and that it was very good (1:31). The expression 'good' (*tov*) becomes 'very good' (*tov meod*). The universe is good. The planet earth is good. The oceans and land are good. All living things are good. Life with its interconnectedness is all very good.

Jesus recognised and marvelled at the beauty of creation:

> Consider the ravens: they neither sow nor reap, they have neither storehouse nor barn, and yet God feeds them. Of how much more value are you than the birds! ... Consider the lilies, how they grow: they neither toil nor spin; yet I tell you, even Solomon in all his glory was not clothed like one of these.
>
> Luke 12:24, 27

What does it mean to say that creation is good when nature can be vicious, cruel, a dog-eat-dog world, with survival of the fittest? Yet God deems it very good. Life as God has created it, is a world of marvels but also challenges, beauty but also trouble, but that is all good. All of it together is very good. It has purpose, meaning, it is ongoing creation that teaches us in its frailty and in its strength.

> For everything created by God is good, and nothing is to be rejected, provided it is received with thanksgiving.
>
> 1 Timothy 4:4

Over the centuries, Christian theology emphasised being saved from 'mourning and weeping in this valley of tears'. Yet this is not a testing place and a passing world. This is reality, with its promises and hopes, joys and splendour. This is where we journey with Christ, in, through and with creation.

As Rabbi Jonathan Sacks explains, to see that someone is good and to say so is one of the great creative acts. To see the good in others and let them see themselves in the mirror of our recognition and praise, is to help someone grow to become better and more creative. This is what God does for us and calls us to do for others.[32]

In this first account of creation, many have interpreted the creation of humans at the end as the pinnacle of God's creation. God creates ever more complex creatures and the final creation is that of humans. However, God does not call humans 'good' at their creation, but only when God looks at humans within the scope of the entire world is it all considered 'very good'. Humans came last because their survival is dependent on a flourishing world. Without the sun and the moon, sea and land, marine life, bird life and animal life, plants and vegetation, the reality is that our human life would be non-existent!

The outcome of every stage in the creative process is declared 'good' by God. It acknowledges creation's integrity and self-sustainability, from seeds to reproduction. The climax of creation, according to William P. Brown, is the seventh day (2:1-3), when God ceases to create, thereby allowing creation, under human 'dominion,' to thrive on its own.[33] So, the 'goodness' of creation includes the gifts of:

---

[32] Rabbi Jonathan Sacks, 'Three Stages of Creation - Covenant & Conversation – Parshah' https://www.chabad.org/parshah/article_cdo/aid/4158654/jewish/Three-Stages-of-Creation.htm

[33] William P. Brown, 'Biblical Accounts of Creation' in *The Old Testament and Ethics. A book-by-book survey.* Joel B. Green and Jacqueline E. Lapsley, Editors, (Grand Rapids, Michigan: Baker Academic, 2013), 166.

- Sabbath rest every seventh day (2:1-3; Exodus 20:8-1)
- Sexuality and procreation among God's creatures (1:22, 28; 2:21-25)
- Provision of abundant food (1:30; 2:9, 16; 9:1-4).

To call creation 'good', however, does not indicate idealised perfection. The primeval and watery forces of chaos and evil (1:2) are not eliminated but pushed to the margin (1:6-7; 7:11). Later in Genesis, we will read that the serpent that tempted humans was made by the Lord God (Genesis 3:1).[34]

Creation comes with the good and the not so good. A world in evolution. A world with twists and turns, on the move with creating and propagating. And yet there arrive moments of slowing down and resting.

> **Genesis 2:2-3** *And on the seventh day God finished the work that he had done, and he rested on the seventh day from all the work that he had done. ³So God blessed the seventh day and hallowed it, because on it God rested from all the work that he had done in creation.*

The Sabbath is called 'rest' because it pertains to mystery, gift, contemplation and being present, just as God becomes present to it all. God's last creative act is not in making humanity, but a period of rest for the sake of humanity and all creatures... the sound of silence following

---

[34] Dennis T. Olsen, 'Genesis' in *The Old Testament and Ethics. A book-by-book survey,'* Joel B Green and Jacqueline E. Lapsley, editors (Grand Rapids: Michigan: Baker Academic, 2013), 44.

creation is very different to the brooding uncertainty before the world's creation.[35]

Sabbath is primarily about re-connection with God and with all creatures in order to allow flourishing and plenitude. Living from the Sabbath leads to transformation of encounter and a deep sensitivity to the created world as Celia Deane-Drummond puts in point form:[36]

1. Give time and space to reaffirming a sense of covenant between God, humanity and creation.
2. Acknowledge the dependence of all creation on God and God's authority over evil and chaos.
3. Acknowledge the contribution of human sinfulness to the destruction and devastation of creation, including loss of biodiversity and the need for metanoia.
4. Move away from those cycles of behaviour that urge more and more economic growth, in favour of a deeper balancing of human activity and rest as integral to that in the natural world.
5. Celebrate the presence of Christ in the midst of creation and acknowledge Christ's redeeming power for all the brokenness in creation, including sinful humanity.

---

[35] Celia Deane-Drummond, 'Living from the Sabbath: Developing and Ecological Theology in the Context of Biodiversity' in *Biodiversity and Ecology as Interdisciplinary Challenge*, Denis Edwards and Mark Worthing Editors, (Adelaide: ATF Press, 2004), 6.

[36] Celia Deane-Drummond, 'Living from the Sabbath: Developing and Ecological Theology in the Context of Biodiversity' 12.

6. Learn to appreciate the value of all creation in and of itself, as God's creation, rather than just a resource for human benefit.
7. Develop a sense of wonder that includes a deep joy in creation as it is now, in all its richness and diversity, as well as what it might become in glory.
8. Acknowledge an ignorance of the complexity of the natural world and develop the virtue of humility, or realistic appreciation of who we are in relationship to creation.
9. Enter into an understanding of creation as manifesting the wisdom of God, and seek to practise wisdom and prudence in our dealings with creation.
10. Learn to love creation as gift, as it is in itself, and as expressive of the love of God.
11. Find ways to recognise and balance competing demands and promote ecological justice.

Later versions of the law of keeping the Sabbath emphasised the social and ethical dimension with the Israelites extending the day of rest to everyone in the society, slave and free alike (Exodus 16:29; 23:12; Deuteronomy 5:12-15, 24:19-21; Leviticus 25:4-7).

[8]Remember the sabbath day, and keep it holy. [9]For six days you shall labour and do all your work. [10]But the seventh day is a sabbath to the LORD your God; you shall not do any work—you, your son or your daughter, your male or female slave, your livestock, or the alien resident in your towns. [11]For in six days the LORD made heaven and earth, the sea, and all that

is in them, but rested the seventh day; therefore the LORD blessed the sabbath day and consecrated it.

Exodus 20:8-11

The Sabbath is a way to living a sustainable life, limiting use of resources one day out of seven. It provides time to evaluate the work for the week, just as God evaluated the making of creation, and it provides space to consider and reflect on the meaning of life.

Once a week, we are called to refrain from all labour that employs the things of nature for the achievement of human ends. Peter Abelard (1079-1142) evoked the glimpse of the end of the journey:

> There Sabbath unto Sabbath
> Succeeds eternally,
> The joy that has no ending
> Of souls in holiday.

The Sabbath is a reminder that creation is worth more than any monetary considerations. Yet, despite the sacredness of Sabbath, Jesus had to contend with people who distorted its meaning (Luke 13:14-16 and Matthew 12:9-12). In contemporary times, Sunday is no longer seen as the day of 'rest', but when we relinquish our rest, we also relinquish our ability to appreciate and give thanks.

Under pressure, pushed and pulled from every direction, voices demanding, deadlines, work and more work, time running out, late hours, noise, busy, busy, busy, must do, no time, meetings, directives, phone calls, emails, texts, come on, hurry up, no time. And there was evening. Too tired to do anything. Exhausted. Sleepy. Mind juggling work and breathed into his nostrils the breath of life; and the man became a living being. [8] And the LORD God planted a garden in Eden, in the east; and there he put the man whom he had formed. [9] Out of the ground the LORD God made to grow every tree that is pleasant to the sight and good for food, the tree of life also in the midst of the garden, and the tree of the knowledge of good and evil.

[10] A river flows out of Eden to water the garden, and from there it divides and becomes four branches. [11] The name of the first is Pishon; it is the one that flows around the whole land of Havilah, where there is gold; [12] and the gold of that land is good; bdellium and onyx stone are there. [13] The name of the second river is Gihon; it is the one that flows around the whole land of Cush. [14] The name of the third river is Tigris, which flows east of Assyria. And the fourth river is the Euphrates.

[15] The LORD God took the man and put him in the garden of Eden to till it and keep it. [16] And the LORD God commanded the man, 'You may freely eat of every tree of the garden; [17] but of the tree of the knowledge of good and evil you shall not eat, for in the day that you eat of it you shall die.'

[18] Then the LORD God said, 'It is not good that the man should be alone; I will make him a helper as his partner.' [19] So out of the ground the LORD God formed every animal of the field and every bird of the air, and brought them to the man to see what he would call them; and whatever the man called each living creature, that was its name. [20] The man gave names to all cattle, and to the birds of the air, and to every animal of the field; but for the man there was not found a helper as his partner. [21] So the LORD God caused a deep sleep to fall upon the man, and he slept; then he took one of his ribs and closed up its place with flesh. [22] And the

rib that the Lord *God had taken from the man he made into a woman and brought her to the man.* ²³*Then the man said,*

> *'This at last is bone of my bones*
> *and flesh of my flesh;*
> *this one shall be called Woman,*
> *for out of Man this one was taken.'*

²⁴*Therefore a man leaves his father and his mother and clings to his wife, and they become one flesh.* ²⁵*And the man and his wife were both naked, and were not ashamed.*

Genesis 2:4b-25

The best way to explain the various inconsistencies and duplications in the books of the Pentateuch is to assume that the books are a redaction, an edited version of several different original sources. This is called the documentary hypothesis, the four-source theory, or the JEPD theory (Yahwist, Elohist, Deuteronomist and Priestly). These four sources have been identified by biblical scholars by their specific literary styles and theological concerns. In the case of the two Genesis creation stories, they have been attributed to the Yahwist and Priestly influences.

J or Yahwist: (The J initial is from the German form of Yahwist.) Originated in the southern kingdom (Judah), perhaps as early as the reigns of King Solomon or King David, it is the earliest source, dating back to the tenth century BCE. The J sections of the Torah are where the Hebrew name for God is YHWH, even in accounts of events before YHWH disclosed the name to Moses in Exodus 3:6. The Yahwist source presents God with human qualities and relates quite naturally to humans. YHWH walks in the garden and talks with the man. The style is smooth, colourful, vivid, dramatic and concise. Examples include the story of creation of man and woman (Genesis 2:4–25) and the Ten Plagues (Exodus 7:14 to 10:29).

P or Priestly source: Thought to have developed during and after the Exile (587–538 BCE), thus it dates around sixth century BCE. The theology of this source is that the Jewish people's religious identity is found in proper worship and special laws that set them apart from other people. Genesis 1 is considered to be the Priestly source and Genesis 2 is considered to be influenced by the Yahwist source. Reasons for this are seen in the styles of writing.

- Humankind appears on the sixth day in the Priestly account, while in the Yahwist account humankind is created immediately after the heavens and the earth and before anything else.
- In the Priestly account, man and woman are created together, while in the Yahwist account woman is made after man and from man.
- God is distant in the Priestly account and creation occurs by the medium of 'and God said'.
- In the Yahwist account, God is an artisan depicted as physically working, almost like a potter with key 'creative' words including, God made, formed, breathed, planted, etc.
- The Priestly account refers to God as Elohim. The Yahwist account refers to God as Yahweh

As we explore the second creation account in the book of Genesis, we will refer to God as the Lord God which is the English translation for Yahweh used in the *New Revised Standard Version of the Bible*.

The second creation story begins with the land barren and dry. No rain and so no green verdure, no lushness and so neither plants nor herbs. The writer understands how fragile the earth is and how vegetation and water are a balancing act, with the importance and value of arable land and heaven-sent rain.

> **Genesis 2:4-6** *In the day that the* LORD *God made the earth and the heavens, ⁵when no plant of the field was yet in the earth and no herb of the field had yet sprung up – for the* LORD *God had not caused it to rain upon the earth, and there was no one to till the ground, but a stream would rise from the earth, and water the whole face of the ground.*

When 'the LORD God had not caused it to rain upon the earth', we know the devastating consequences – with drought-stricken areas, no crops, out of control bushfires, dying cattle, and then the resulting impact of soaring meat, vegetables and fruit prices. We are at the mercy of nature. We need the rains to come down and the sun to shine; otherwise, fertility is non-existent.

The Lord God had made the earth and the heavens but no rain and so no vegetation. It is a desolate scene, painted in silence, lacking colour. And then we read that a stream would rise and water the ground. It is a word of hope and trust. The Lord God does not abandon creation. When all seems dry and dead, there is still possibility of life.

> ¹⁵*When the water in the skin was gone, she cast the child under one of the bushes.* ¹⁶*Then she went and sat down opposite him a good way off, about*

the distance of a bowshot; for she said, 'Do not let me look on the death of the child'. And as she sat opposite him, she lifted up her voice and wept. [17] And God heard the voice of the boy; and the angel of God called to Hagar from heaven, and said to her, 'What troubles you, Hagar? Do not be afraid; for God has heard the voice of the boy where he is. [18] Come, lift up the boy and hold him fast with your hand, for I will make a great nation of him'. [19] Then God opened her eyes, and she saw a well of water. She went, and filled the skin with water, and gave the boy a drink.

Genesis 21:15-19

Then Moses lifted up his hand and struck the rock twice with his staff; water came out abundantly, and the congregation and their livestock drank.

Numbers 20:11
(see also Isaiah 55:1, 10-11 and John 7:37-38)

Water is life-giving and can be sourced even in the driest of places. Hidden in our world is the life blood that we need. Waters will rise, to quench our thirsts.

Aside from the image of water, the word 'ground' also occurs a number of times in the second account of creation.

2:5 – there was no one to till the ground
2:6 – and water the whole face of the ground
2:7 – then the Lord God formed man from the dust of the ground
2:19 – So out of the ground the Lord God formed every animal

The ground is key to life. This ground we emerge from, walk on, work on, live on and are buried in. As humans, we are 'grounded'. We are dependent upon this ground that we tread. This ground that provides us with all we need, or, as God reminds Moses, 'the place on which you are standing is holy ground' (Exodus 3:5).

In Genesis 2:5, the narrator uses the word *'adamah* which was first mentioned in 1:25 as the earth/soil upon which all other life crawls. Humanity is thus the *'adam* taken from the *'adamah* – an earth creature taken from the earth.

Genesis 2:7 *then the* LORD *God formed man from the dust of the ground, and breathed into his nostrils the breath of life; and the man became a living being.*

In ancient accounts of how humans were created, they are often born of the earth:

- Sumerian myth of *Enki* and *Ninmah* – 'Namma then kneaded some clay, placed it in her womb, and gave birth to the first humans'.
- In the Babylonian and the Mesopotamian myth of *Atrahasis* – 'Nintu shall mix clay with his flesh and his blood. Then a god and a man will be mixed together in clay'.
- Egyptian potter god, Khnum, fashions gods and humans on his potter's wheel – 'He fashioned them of clay with the air of his potter's wheel'.
- In *Enuma Elish*, the god Marduk announces to the goddess Ea that he will form a 'man' to be created 'to perform hard agricultural labour for the gods'. Humanity was slave labour for the gods in these ancient accounts.

Genesis 2:7 is the making of a man and affirms that humans were created to be in relationship with the LORD God, not to be subordinates. The *Adam* is formed from the dust of the *Adamah*. So, humankind came from the earth, formed like a pottery figure.

> ³So I went down to the potter's house, and there he was working at his wheel. ⁴The vessel he was making of clay was spoiled in the potter's hand, and he reworked it into another vessel, as seemed good to him.
> ⁵Then the word of the LORD came to me: ⁶Can I not do with you, O house of Israel, just as this potter has done? says the LORD. Just like the clay in the potter's hand, so are you in my hand, O house of Israel.
>
> Jeremiah 18:3-6

In the first creation account, there is no effort on the part of God who simply speaks. God says, 'Let there be', and there was. In the second, the Lord God is actively engaged. When it comes to the creation of the first human, the Lord God performs the creation, like a sculptor fashioning an image out of clay. As Peter Varengo writes:

> Clay – amorphous mass, ordinary, cheap and common. Yet there is nothing cheap and common for the potter who discovers beauty and potential and preciousness within the amorphous commonality. Our high-tech, assembly-line proactivity has lost the sense of relationship that the artisan feels and lives with the object and materials of their work. It is not thus for Jeremiah's potter. He sees beauty within, and he feels the moral imperative to release such

beauty. However, that release is so painful, slow, unrelenting pain, uncontrollable by the clay itself. Cutting, tearing, shaping, beating, spinning, and spinning over and over again.[38]

Jane N. Dowling notes that the term 'Dust of the ground' conjures up images of filth, dirt, scum and rubbish. These images often arise for survivors of sexual abuse and we translate them into words by telling others we feel like 'dirt', 'crap', 'rubbish', or 'shit'!'[39] Dowling's comments are a timely reminder that how we see ourselves and others is linked to how we have been formed and supported.

Yet, the Lord God not only 'formed man from the dust of the ground' (Genesis 2:7), but 'breathed into his nostrils the breath of life', indicating that God is the Creator of physical and spiritual life. This *Adam* was not a living being until the Lord God breathed into the figure, which then became a *nephesh*, a living being or soul.

> The hand of the LORD came upon me, and he brought me out by the spirit of the LORD and set me down in the middle of a valley; it was full of bones. ²He led me all round them; there were very many lying in the valley, and they were very dry. ³He said to me, 'Mortal, can these bones live?' I answered, 'O LORD God, you know'. ⁴Then he said to me, 'Prophesy to

---

[38] Peter Varengo, *You are the Kingdom. An exploration of discipleship through the Gospel imagery of the Kingdom as Divine Presence in the World*, (Victoria, Australia: Coventry Press, 2020), 165.

[39] Jane N. Dowling, *Come Forward! Bold enough to heal. A Spiritual Handbook for survivors of sexual abuse using Scripture, Visualisation and Art Therapy*, (Victoria, Australia: Coventry Press, 2019), 24.

these bones, and say to them: O dry bones, hear the word of the LORD. ⁵Thus says the LORD God to these bones: I will cause breath to enter you, and you shall live. ⁶I will lay sinews on you, and will cause flesh to come upon you, and cover you with skin, and put breath in you, and you shall live; and you shall know that I am the LORD.'

Ezekiel 37:1-6

The breath of life – to breathe, to live. To stop breathing. To die. We breathe without even being aware of it. It is gentle, quiet, unnoticed, but it is life-giving. Lord God creates gently, tenderly and with love. We are brought to life, touched, blessed and graced and we now share intimately in God's life. Can we call it the kiss of life! Maybe so as Richard Rohr explains:

> the consonants used in the word *Yahweh* are the Hebrew consonants that do not allow us to close our lips or use our tongue. In fact the sacred name *Yahweh* is an attempt to imitate and replicate the sound of inhalation and exhalation... The word that archetypal religion came up with for God, for the great I AM, was a word mimicking breath itself, unspeakable because it is only breathable... It is the same air we all breathe, and yet each of us receives it intimately. No one controls it!... Simply inhale, *Yah*, and exhale, *weh*, with mouth open, lips and tongue relaxed.[40]

---

[40] Richard Rohr, *Dancing Standing Still. Healing the world from a place of prayer*, (New York: Paulist Press, 2014), 28.

The Lord God is in the very air we breathe and our breathing is continual. We need to breathe each moment. We are one with God with each breath we take.

So, if we imagine the very first 'breath of Life' that God breathed into us, we may imagine God breathing the Lord God's own Life in us – Love. Yet as Jane N. Dowling draws to our attention, 'I am aware that for some survivors of sexual abuse, the phrase "breath of life" may trigger some traumatic memories, depending on the individual's context of sexual abuse'.[41] We need to be mindful of how we relate to others and how we present the Lord God's loving kindness.

We are made from the kiss of life. We are gently created, softly caressed, tenderly awakened, loved into life, blessed by the Lord God. And on our last breath out, we die. The following is a reflection by Bob Holmes that contemplates the breath of life:

> Your breath recreates us
> with welcoming
> Acceptance,
> Belonging
> Wrapped
> in your eternal embrace of love,
> we are whole
> Time falls away
> becoming timeless
> as we enter the dance
> being woven with the threads of eternal life
> that eternal character and love of God

---

[41] Dowling, *Come Forward! Bold enough to heal. A Spiritual Handbook for survivors of sexual abuse using Scripture, Visualisation and Art Therapy*, 30.

coursing through our very heart, soul, and sinew
transforming the very earth we walk upon
with heaven
bearing the presence of God

>As We Breathe The Breath of Heaven
>by Bob Holmes #comeintothequiet

So, we are created gently and lovingly. Awakening to life, we are welcomed into wonder and beauty. We are also awakened to a reality that calls us to see, know and live fully.

Genesis 2:8 *And the* Lord *God planted a garden in Eden, in the east; and there he put the man whom he had formed.*

In Genesis 1, God effortlessly summons the universe into being. In Genesis 2, the Lord God becomes a gardener, 'Now the Lord God planted a garden'. This is not a foreign concept in the Bible with Jesus being identified as a gardener in John 20:15. Jesus also makes reference to God as a gardener in John 15:1-2 and speaks parables which tell of sowing seeds and tilling in Luke (8:4-8, 13:6-9, 18-19).

The Hebrew word *'eden* means 'delight' or 'pleasure'. The Hebrew word *gan* or 'garden' refers to a fenced off enclosure protected by a wall or hedge. The garden of Eden is therefore a special place that is spatially separated from the outside world. It is a fertile, well-watered place that is constantly cared for.[42]

---

[42] Dumbrell, *Covenant and Creation. An Old Testament Covenant Theology*, 38.

In archetypal literature, a garden is a place of delight, the place of love, the place to drink wine, the place where lovers meet in the moonlight, the place of intimacy.

> O you who dwell in the gardens,
>   my companions are listening for your voice;
>   let me hear it.
>
> Song of Songs 8:13 (see also 5:1; 6:2; 7:12-13)

The garden is a paradise, a token of divine care, an ideal world to be realised, where we hear God's voice and experience God's presence. The garden of Eden is any place we can feel at home, a place where we are intimate with God. Our garden of Eden is a place we can be as we really are, with no pressure to keep up appearances. We are free to roam where we want, how we want, and when we want. The garden, our world, is meant to be our home and playground, our delight and pleasure.

> For the Lord will comfort Zion; he will comfort all her waste places, and will make her wilderness like Eden, her desert like the garden of the Lord; joy and gladness will be found in her, thanksgiving and the voice of song.
>
> Isaiah 51:3

Before the expulsion from the garden, what did woman and man do there? What was their paradise like? What do we name as our paradise? Given some thought, we would veer towards times of carefree joy, of beauty and wonder, of excitement and enthusiasm, of laughter, of friendships and fun. Paradise is our heartfelt landscape, the place we can be wonderfully away, and yet also to be a way of presence, that is in harmony with God's beautiful desires.

Immediately upon creating the man, the Lord God gets excited and 'planted a garden in Eden'. The Lord God puts the man there for drab and dull was not meant for us. We are to venture on, warmed by sun, chilled by wind, God ever so close, ever so far. We gaze at God, return the look, remember and go on.

As long as God walks with us, we recognise the world to be blessed, beautiful, graced and very good. But we lose the sense of paradise when we take God out of it.

However, it would be foolish to think that we can just live in paradise all our lives. Even in paradise, there is work to be done – tilling and keeping. Paradise is not some imaginary distant fantasy land. It is here and now with its beauty but also its demands.

It is up to us if we see our life as one of paradise or one of dust. How we see life is how we choose to live it. Can we accept the garden with all its beauty and temptations?

> I am the sound of bird's song greeting the
> Dawn.
> The rustle of wind caressing the Pines.
> The glint of sunlight tapping the path through the woods.
> The Creek trickling slowly but steadily to the lake.
>
> I am...
> In the embrace of life savouring the love of
> Ancient friends.

Cynthia Helton

Our garden planet, our paradise, our home. We belong gently to this earth and the earth gifts itself to us.

> **Genesis 2:9** *Out of the ground the* Lord *God made to grow every tree that is pleasant to the sight and good for food...*

Humans have been placed in the garden of Eden, revelling in its pleasures, where the Lord God provided 'every tree that is pleasant to the sight and good for food'.

The Lord God has planted trees that are pleasant to the sight and good for food. The first description is 'pleasant to the sight' and following from it is, 'good for food'. The order matters. The Lord God sees the beauty of things and the eating comes later. Humans, however, have a tendency to hungrily see the usefulness of things and forget about their natural beauty. As Thomas Merton insightfully wrote:

> A tree gives glory to God first of all by being a tree... the perfection of each created thing is not merely in its conformity to an abstract type but in its own individual identity with itself. This particular tree will give glory to God by spreading out its roots and raising its branches into the air and light in a way that no other tree before or after it ever did or will do.[43]

In our biblical creation story, we have a garden with every tree to admire. More so, we have the planting of the tree of life and lastly the tree of knowledge of good and evil. Therefore, the order is:

---

[43] Thomas Merton, New Seeds of Contemplation, (New York: A New Directions Book, 1972), 29.

- Pleasing
- Food
- Life
- Knowledge

Food is a need but when it consumes us, we lose the joy of eating. Food is nourishment but it is also noticing the colours and smells and tastes on offer. To eat we must first plant and in planting we intimately know the land, vegetation and that all life needs nourishing.

Noticing what 'is pleasant to the sight' would save the world a great deal of trouble. To stop and see, appreciate and value, delight in what is given, and maybe then we would not be so quick to tear things apart to satisfy our desires.

> Meanwhile the world goes on.
> Meanwhile the sun and the clear pebbles of the rain
> are moving across the landscapes,
> over the prairies and the deep trees,
> the mountains and the rivers.
> Meanwhile the wild geese, high in the clean blue air,
> are heading home again.
> Whoever you are, no matter how lonely,
> the world offers itself to your imagination,
> calls to you like the wild geese, harsh and exciting —
> over and over announcing your place
> in the family of things.
>
> *Wild Geese* by Mary Oliver[44]

---

[44] Mary Oliver, *Devotions: The Selected Poems of Mary Oliver*, (New York: Penguin Books, 2020).

Creation and creating is about noticing and engaging in the actual moment. It is to be consumed in the knowledge of the present and to be a part of what is before us.

Genesis 2:9 *The tree of life also in the midst of the garden, and the tree of the knowledge of good and evil.*

The two trees in the garden, 'the tree of life' and 'the tree of knowledge of good and evil' represent the unmerited gifts of fullness of life and morality, which distinguish humans from the animal kingdom. In the Sumero-Akkadian myths, only 'the tree of life' is mentioned. It is the Hebrew author, notes Rui de Menzes, who raises the theme of morality. Humans are created free and, as a consequence of this freedom, morality arises. For where there is no freedom there can be no morality, only instinct.[45] Mark Coleridge, further reflects:

> The tree of life is found in all the creation stories of the ancient world that gave us the Bible; but the tree of knowledge is a uniquely biblical planting. This is because, for the most part, the ancient world understood the difference between the gods and human beings as a difference of life: the gods lived for ever and human beings did not. It was a simple difference between mortality and immortality. The gods were neither better nor worse than us; they knew neither more nor less; they simply lived longer. In the Bible, however, the relationship between God and the human being is understood differently. It

---

[45] Rui de Menezes, *The Global vision of the Hebrew Bible*, (Mumbai: St Pauls, 2009), 37.

is not so much a difference of mortality but a difference of knowledge. God knows everything and we do not; and we must leave behind the world of ignorance and journey towards the knowledge God alone possesses, without ever thinking that we shall know as God knows. In particular, only God knows the difference between good and evil. For the human being to claim the right to decide what is good and what is evil is, according to the Book of Genesis, the very heart of what it means to play God. It is the root-sin of the human race. That is why the tree that really matters in Paradise is not the tree of life but the tree of knowledge.

In other words, when the human being plays God by claiming the right to decide what is evil and what is good, the inevitable consequence is death of one kind or another.[46]

Knowledge of both good and evil exist at the time of human creation, there in the garden, accessible to humans, in the same locale. So the Lord God is credited with generating the precondition for human evil in the form of knowledge of it.[47]

Humankind is forbidden to eat fruit from the tree of knowledge of good and evil on the pain of death (2:17). There is no prohibition established on eating the fruit of the tree of life. The tree of life is for us to take from. God does not prohibit our approach.

---

[46] Mark Coleridge, *Words from The Wound*, (Strathfield, NSW: St Pauls Publications, 2014), 254.

[47] Mark S. Smith, 'Before Human Sin and Evil: Desire and Fear in the Garden of God,' in *The Catholic Biblical Quarterly*, Vol 80, 2018:221.

> I call heaven and earth to witness against you today that I have set before you life and death, blessings and curses. Choose life so that you and your descendants may live.
>
> Deuteronomy 30:19

> I came that they may have life, and have it abundantly.
>
> John 10:10

People have always desired prolonged life, if not eternal life. But life is never ending. Life is here and now, given to be lived, and in our own death, our spirit goes on forever. God creates, always creating, neither to forget, nor to destroy, nor to obliterate, but to embrace and love. We are continually becoming, deepening, enjoying and celebrating who we are. And as we continue with the creation narrative, we are immersed in the landscape of our whereabouts.

> **Genesis 2:10-14** *A river flows out of Eden to water the garden, and from there it divides and becomes four branches. ¹¹The name of the first is Pishon; it is the one that flows around the whole land of Havilah, where there is gold; ¹²and the gold of that land is good; bdellium and onyx stone are there. ¹³The name of the second river is Gihon; it is the one that flows around the whole land of Cush. ¹⁴The name of the third river is Tigris, which flows east of Assyria. And the fourth river is the Euphrates.*

The name of four great rivers: Pishon, Gihon, Tigris and Euphrates. The passage might feel like a later insertion in the Creation account, but nothing, as we all know, is without meaning and purpose.

- Gerhard von Rad thinks the inclusion of the rivers in the narrative was for the purpose of indicating Eden's physical location.
- Walter Brueggemann sees Genesis 2:10–14 as the intrusion of a disparate tradition into the text, and although he notices that the text has a parallel in Ezekiel 47:1-12, he concludes that, 'The rivers play no part in the Genesis narrative' (Brueggemann 1982).
- Water has been brought under control from a previous state of chaos, subsequently ordered in such a way by God that will nurture growth and fertility (Bechtel 1993).
- The symmetrical and orderly description of the four rivers runs directly counter to the waters/deep in Genesis 1:2 that are symbolic of death and chaos. Whereas disordered waters are chaos/death archetypes, ordered waters are life/growth archetypes. The four rivers can be understood as symbols of order, maturity and completeness.[48]

Rivers mean life and sustainability and without them there is no water, no vegetation and no survival. Natural landmarks are important and vital to identity. The course of rivers divides the land and marks out territory to determine where one settles, where one farms and where one can fish. The features of the land have a long history to tell. The

---

[48] David James Stewart, 'The emergence of consciousness in Genesis 1–3: Jung's depth psychology and theological anthropology,' in *Zygon*, vol. 49, no. 2 (June 2014), 521.

four rivers in this biblical creation account have weaved and furrowed and swirled their way into the imagination.

Rivers, ever flowing, tumbling, tossing, watering, spraying, eroding, bursting, meandering and always creating and recreating the landscape of the earth and of our hearts and minds.

> We go to the sea at night and stand along the shore. We listen to the urgent roll of the waves reaching ever higher until they reach their limits and can go no farther, then return to an inward peace until the moon calls again for their presence on these shores. So it is with a fulfilling vision that we may attain – for a brief moment. Then it is gone, only to return again in the deepening awareness of a presence that holds all things together.[49]

Rivers, part of creation, bursting forth to give life and to also draw us back into the deep mystery. Ebbing and flowing in and out of life. Yet we dam the rivers or re-direct their course so that we leave settlement areas without a life blood. We pollute the waterways and choke them of all life. We drain the rivers leaving a dry bone bed, where once a might waterway tumbled and tossed.

Humans are called to live on the land, to treat the place as a paradise. It is not to forsake and destroy, but to create and nurture.

---

[49] Thomas Berry, *The Sacred Universe. Earth, Spirituality, and Religion in the Twenty-First Century*, edited by Mary Evelyn Tucker, (New York: Columbia University Press, 2009), 176-177.

Genesis 2:15 *The LORD God took the man and put him in the garden of Eden to till it and keep it.*

In Genesis 2:15, the Hebrew word for till is *abad*, and the Hebrew word for keep is *shamar* (2:5, 15; 3:23). These words are also used to describe how the priests cared for the tabernacle of Moses.

> Thus they shall keep charge of the tent of meeting and the sanctuary, and shall attend the descendants of Aaron, their kindred, for the service of the house of the LORD.
>
> 1 Chronicles 23:32
> (see also Numbers 3:7-8; 8:25-26;
> Ezekiel 44:14; Isaiah 56:6)

'Tilling' refers to cultivating, ploughing or working, while 'keeping' means caring, protecting, overseeing and preserving. So the relationship in Eden between humankind and other creatures is one of caretakers of creation, given a task and responsibility.

> This we know... all things are connected like the blood which unites one family. All things are connected. Whatever befalls the earth befalls the sons of the earth. Man does not weave the web of life, he is merely a strand in it. Whatever he does to the web, he does to himself. When the last red man has vanished from this earth, and his memory is only a shadow of a cloud moving across the prairie, those shores and forests will still hold the spirits of my people. For they love this earth as the new-born loves its mother's heartbeat. So if we sell our land, love it as we've loved

it. Care for it as we've cared for it. Hold in your mind the memory of the land as it is when you take it. And with all your strength, with all your mind, with all your heart, preserve it for your children and love it... as God loves us all. One thing we know. Our God is the same God.... Even the white man cannot be exempt from the common destiny. We may be brothers after all. We shall see.

Chief Seattle, 1854
http://www.barefootsworld.net/seattle.html

Paul Tillich notes that humans have to shape the world and themselves, according to the productive powers given to them. Creative individuals, geniuses... were inspired by this idea of participation in the creative process of the universe... enthusiasm and rationality were united. The courage was both the courage to be as oneself and the courage to be as a part.[50]

'To till and keep' is hard labour, but will yield abundance. Time devoted to beautifying and nurturing life. A task that requires dedication and time. A labour that benefits one and all. Effort that requires the natural elements to play a role. If we took the words 'to till' practically and seriously, we would discover the richness of this earth and that what grows is treasure for our lives.

'To keep' means to look after. However, to keep also means to maintain in one's possession. Perhaps God meant both to look after and to keep close to one's heart. It becomes our responsibility and our concern. The world is ours to

---

[50] Paul Tillich, *The Courage to Be*, (London: Yale University Press, 2000), 104-105.

have, to keep. We claim it as our own because it means something to us. We draw it close to us for safe-keeping. And we see this in the way people become so attached to their block of land and their house. They own that piece of God's land, that place they call home. It nurtures them and they nurture it. They keep it with delight. John Hattie and Klaus Zierer refer to the IKEA effect which can also be applied to the land.

> It is not easy to assemble a bookshelf out of the thousands of parts you get when you buy a flat pack. People who succeed in doing it value the IKEA bookshelf more highly than an expensive piece of antique furniture. This is because we have a higher value for things we are involved in creating or solving – it is a product of all the effort and hard work it took to put the bookshelf together.[51]

In tilling and keeping, we come to value more highly the land given to us to recreate. And when we see the fruits of our efforts, to till and keep, our hunger for responsibility is better understood and accepted.

> A farmer has no time to be bored. There is no emptiness in his life, it is all fullness. You have only to look at the varied round of the year's work – and what work! Work that does truly elevate the spirit, to say nothing of its variety. In it, a man goes hand in hand with nature, with the seasons of the year, and is in touch and in sympathy with

---

[51] John Hattie and Klaus Zierer, *10 Mindframes for Visible Learning. Teaching for success*, (London: Routledge, 2018), 135.

everything that is done in creation. Before the spring is here, our labours are already beginning: there is carting and getting in timber, and while the roads are impassable, there is the getting ready the seed, the sifting and measuring of the corn in the granaries and the drying of it and distributing the tasks among the peasants. As soon as the snows and floods are over, work begins in earnest; by the river there is loading the boats, then there is thinning trees in the wood and planting trees in the garden, and in every direction the men are turning up the ground. The spade is at work in the vegetable garden, the ploughs and harrows in the fields. And the sowing begins – that's a trifling matter of course: they are sowing the future harvest! When summer has come, there's the mowing, the husbandman's first holiday – that's a trifling matter too! One harvest comes after the other, after the rye the wheat, after the barley the oats, and then the pulling of the hemp. They throw the hay into cocks, they build the stacks. And when August is half over, there is the carting of it all to the threshing barns. Autumn comes, there is the ploughing and the sowing of the winter corn, the repair of the granaries, the barns and the cattle-sheds, sampling the corn, and the first threshing. Winter comes and even then work does not flag: the first wagon-loads setting off for the town, threshing in all the barns, the carting of the threshed grain from the barns to the granaries; in the woods, the chopping and sawing of timber, the carting of bricks and materials for the building in the spring... It's in this, just in this, that a man imitates God. God chose for Himself the work of creation as the highest delight, and requires the same of man, that he should be the creator of prosperity and the harmonious order of things. And they call that dull work!'

Nikolai Gogol[52]

Nikolai Gogol adeptly describes the toil but also the joy of deep engagement with the land.

And yet what comes next is extremely important. This is the first time in the Bible that God speaks to humans.

> **Genesis 2:16-17** *And the* LORD *God commanded the man, 'You may freely eat of every tree of the garden but of the tree of the knowledge of good and evil you shall not eat, for in the day that you eat of it you shall die.*

The first words out of the Lord God's mouth are positive, not negative. God speaks 'yes' before 'no'.[53] 'You may freely eat of every tree of the garden.' Freely eat, roam, explore, discover, enjoy, venture forth, be amazed. Test it, try it. What an important line and top of the notch gift! The Lord God has given us the freedom to grow, learn and discover the sights, tastes and sounds of the world. We have understated this one line, all too focused on the verse that follows. Yet this line is significant to us.

Through verses 15 to 17, the Lord God gives possibilities for us in the garden of Eden.

---

[52] Nikolai Gogol, *Dead Souls*, Penguin Classics, Part 2: Chapter 3: 208-210 https://en.wikisource.org/wiki/Dead_Souls—A_Poem/Book_Two/Chapter_III

[53] Leonard Sweet and Frank Viola, Jesus. A Theography, (Nashville: Thomas Nelson, 2012), 45.

1. Put him in the garden – this is where we belong. We are created to live life. The Lord God wants us here.
2. To till it – we need to work in order to create. Sowing comes before reaping. Each one of us has a task to do in life.
3. Keep it – the Lord God wants us to care for this world as much as the Lord God looked upon it and recognised its value.
4. Freely eat – enjoy the gifts of creation. Feed your fantasy, satisfy your curiosity, nourish your mind and appease your hunger.
5. But… you shall not – there are limits to what we can and cannot do, to what we know and do not know. We need to be careful we do not replace good with evil, create chaos out of order.

In summary we are called to:

- Live
- Work
- Care
- Enjoy
- Discern

The first commandment in the Bible is, 'Eat freely'. The last commandment in the Bible is, 'Let anyone who desires drink freely from the water of life' (Revelation 22:17). So 'taste and see that the Lord is good' (Psalm 34:8).

Freely eat of every tree as there is plenty of good things generously given. If we took the time to explore, to taste and see the goodness, to delight in every tree, then we would not be so pre-occupied with the one prohibition, not to eat of the tree of knowledge of good and evil. God has kindled the curiosity and hunger of humans by providing a world (garden) of every tree.

'You shall' suggests the Lord God gives clear directions of right and wrong and yet due to freedom of thought and action, we can be influenced by temptation that makes us question and desire. It is God alone who distinguishes between good and evil and the one who holds all beings accountable. God provided humans with a choice of whether or not to acquire the knowledge of evil, since they already knew good. God opened up the possibility of evil, but in doing so God validated choice.[54] To eat of the fruit of 'good and evil' is to unite oneself to 'good and evil', and to 'know' it personally.

---

[54] Bible Commentary. Produced by Theology of Work (TOW) Project. 'Genesis 1-11 and Work' https://www.theologyofwork.org/old-testament/genesis-1-11-and-work

Chapter 6

For we are not alone

Genesis 2:18-25

[18] Then the Lord God said, 'It is not good that the man should be alone; I will make him a helper as his partner.' [19] So out of the ground the Lord God formed every animal of the field and every bird of the air, and brought them to the man to see what he would call them; and whatever the man called each living creature, that was its name. [20] The man gave names to all cattle, and to the birds of the air, and to every animal of the field; but for the man there was not found a helper as his partner. [21] So the Lord God caused a deep sleep to fall upon the man, and he slept; then he took one of his ribs and closed up its place with flesh. [22] And the rib that the Lord God had taken from the man he made into a woman and brought her to the man. [23] Then the man said,

> 'This at last is bone of my bones
>   and flesh of my flesh;
> this one shall be called Woman,
>   for out of Man this one was taken.'

[24] Therefore a man leaves his father and his mother and clings to his wife, and they become one flesh. [25] And the man and his wife were both naked, and were not ashamed.

It is not good to be alone. Loneliness haunts us. It casts a sorry figure and a sad shadow. To have been given all of creation but not to be able to share it with another. Loneliness strips one of life, of pleasure, of love. We need others, we crave companionship, a friend to go to, someone to chat with, another to spend time with, a partner to accompany us.

Genesis 2:18 *Then the* LORD *God said, 'It is not good that the man should be alone; I will make him a helper as his partner'.*

Loneliness is becoming one of the largest issues in Western society. Despite over population, and connecting with the world via social media, we are more alone than ever. And more sorry for it.

It is not good that we are always on our own. We begin to lose self confidence, we lack another perspective, we are not challenged, and we become so fixated with ourselves. Yet being alone is also important. Learning to love the silence and one's own company provides time and space for us to notice the little things in life. Covid-19 lockdowns showed us how it can be a blessing to have quiet time alone but it also revealed how much more we need others. Socialising is the life blood of existence. To really be who I am, I need to be with others.

The Lord God feels for the existential isolation of the first man and so creates 'A helper as his partner', the Hebrew word being *'ezer kenegdo.*

- The word *'ezer* is a noun that means 'help, rescue'. It occurs twenty-one times in the Hebrew Scriptures, with fifteen of these referring to the salvation that comes from God. In Psalm 20:1-2 we read, 'May he send you help (*'ezer*) from the sanctuary and give you support from Zion'.
- The word *kenegdo* literally means, 'according to what is in front of' or 'corresponding to'. It is made up of *ke* which means 'as' or 'like,' and *neged*, which means 'opposite' 'against' or 'in front of'. The pronoun suffix *–o*, means 'him'.

Together, the words *'ezer kenegdo* mean, 'a help corresponding to himself' or 'equal and adequate to himself'. As Barbara E. Reid explains, this phrase describes the equal partnership, mutual strength and correspondence that God designed for woman and man.[55]

The intention in creating woman and man was for a partnership of equals. To help and be by the side of the other. To work together, corresponding capabilities, mutuality, an understanding of each other and treated on an equal footing. God wanted the woman and man to collaborate, to work and achieve together, to help and aid one another to fullness of life. There is neither subordination of woman, nor superiority of man. In contrast, both were expected to till and keep, work and create, toil and take responsibility for.

---

[55] Barbara E. Reid, *Wisdom's Feast. An Invitation to Feminist Interpretation of the Scriptures*, (Grand Rapids, Michigan: William B. Eerdmans Publishing Company, 2016), 20.

Genesis 2:19-20 *So out of the ground the* LORD *God formed every animal of the field and every bird of the air, and brought them to the man to see what he would call them; and whatever the man called each living creature, that was its name.* ²⁰*The man gave names to all cattle, and to the birds of the air, and to every animal of the field; but for the man there was not found a helper as his partner.*

In the first creation account, God does all the speaking and humans say nought. In the second creation account, the Lord God commands the man in 2:16. This is followed with the Lord God speaking to the man in 2:18. And now the man speaks for the first time in 2:19.

In chapter 3, we have the serpent speak, the woman and man take turns to speak and then the Lord God speaks. The serpent is then silenced by the Lord God and humans are left silent before the Lord God who has the last word.

To speak is to create. Right from the very beginning of Genesis, words are used to create life. When the Lord God speaks to the man, it is words of generosity but also instruction. The first words humans speak are creative and informative – naming animals, giving voice to their identity and uniqueness.

The gift of speaking is a privilege, an expression of thought, an ability to comprehend and a process of expressing the happenings around us. To name what needs to be named in order that reality proceeds.

Naming is an act of creation. In Genesis 1, God names what God makes, for example, 'God called the light Day, and the darkness Night' (1:5). Other acts of creation are followed by the naming of sky (1:8), earth and seas (1:10).

When the Lord God asks the man to name the animals in the second creation account, the Lord God shares what has been a divine prerogative. To invite humans to name the animals is for us to discover more about the life forms that we inhabit the earth with and to accommodate not only for our needs but for the needs of each named and known living creature.

When we know the name of another, the distance between the two shortens. We are no longer strangers but stand on familiarity. The Lord God 'formed every animal of the field and every bird of the air and brought them to the man to see what he would call them' (2:19). We are trusted with creation, to name, identify and recognise things as they are and offer them their rightful place.

As Julien C. H. Smith and T. Laine Scales note, the man's naming of the animals is evidence of the need to bring order to creation as a constitutive aspect of the task given to humankind. In order to properly exercise dominion, man first had to gain the love, admiration and respect for creation that God possessed intrinsically. These sentiments are reinforced in the act of naming; humans naturally give names to those things that are dear, whether children or pets. Human rule should imitate divine rule.[56]

An affinity exists between us and the rest of creation if we permit ourselves to draw closer. The Lord God creates animals and birds and 'brought them to the man'. Of course, none of these living creatures would suit as a helper and

---

[56] Julien C. H. Smith and T. Laine Scales, 'Stewardship: A Biblical Model for the Formation of Christian Scholars,' in *JECB* 17:1 (2013), 84, 86.

partner (2:20) but they are also neither to be forgotten nor disregarded. To bring them to the man is to understand that:

- Our life is intermingled with the life of all else on the planet
- We are to draw closer and acknowledge other life forms
- To come to better understand creation and its purpose
- To develop an understanding in relation to other living creatures
- To understand that all living creatures have intrinsic value
- That living creatures can offer us comfort and assistance

Everyday, new species are discovered, creation begets new life. We are meant to be in a constant process of discovering and acknowledging it by name. Unfortunately, everyday humans speed up the rate of extinction of species, their names never to be said again. God begets and humans destroy! When did destruction cloud our thoughts?

In the second account of Creation, upon forming the man, the Lord God:

- Put man in the garden 2:8
- Put the man to till and keep it 2:15
- Commanded the man 2:16
- Brought animals to the man to name them 2:19
- Made woman and brought her to the man 2:22

Animals that initially were presented for the role of *ezer* failed to qualify. The fact that they were, like Adam, created out of the dirt, put them literally under his already created feet. Adam's 'companion' (*ezer*) was fashioned differently. To create a genuinely new *ezer* for Adam, there was only one raw resource that met the criterion: *adam*. The ultimate partner would come from the same source.[57]

Yet unlike naming the animals that were brought to him, the man does not name the woman until much later (3:20). It was only after he really came to know her, that the man could name the woman. Instead, when woman is first brought to the man, he recognises her as one with him, equal and much loved. He has no dominion over her.

To name is to call out the identity of that before us, to use the gift of words to bring to life and understanding and to say what matters and thus to re-create. Yet naming has at times been an opportunity to name and shame, an exercise in verbal bullying, a practice in belittling and diminishing. The Lord God calls us to say what must be declared and speak creative truth for all life to grow and flourish. To name the reality before our eyes is to recognise the potential before us and befriend what God has given. Words spoken with creative love opens up a world of new possibilities

Alone, we speak what we understand. In company, we hear others and sing a different tune. It is this different song that the Lord God chooses us to sing.

---

[57] Leonard Sweet and Frank Viola, Jesus. A Theography, (Nashville: Thomas Nelson, 2012), 48.

Genesis 2:21-22 *So the LORD God caused a deep sleep to fall upon the man, and he slept; then he took one of his ribs and closed up its place with flesh. ²²And the rib that the LORD God had taken from the man he made into a woman and brought her to the man.*

A deep sleep and what would follow while the man slept was the pain of birthing new life. Sleep is given to us as a time to rest, to be lost to all around us, our time to stop and allow God to work through us. Despite our passivity, sleep is a time of serious activity on God's part.

It is a painful time (took one of his ribs) but also healing time (closed up its place with flesh). Sleep can be troublesome, but it is also the only time we can allow life to play out uninterrupted.

And there was evening and there was morning... another day. What hopes we hold for another day. What will come our way? For the man, it was awakening to the presence of another, a companion. For Jacob, his eyes awakened to God.

²⁴Jacob was left alone; and a man wrestled with him until daybreak. ²⁵When the man saw that he did not prevail against Jacob, he struck him on the hip socket; and Jacob's hip was put out of joint as he wrestled with him. ²⁶Then he said, 'Let me go, for the day is breaking'. But Jacob said, 'I will not let you go, unless you bless me'. ²⁷So he said to him, 'What is your name?' And he said, 'Jacob'. ²⁸Then the man said, 'You shall no longer be called Jacob, but Israel, for you have striven with God and with humans, and have prevailed'. ²⁹Then Jacob asked him, 'Please

tell me your name'. But he said, 'Why is it that you ask my name?' And there he blessed him. [30]So Jacob called the place Peniel, saying, 'For I have seen God face to face, and yet my life is preserved'. [31]The sun rose upon him as he passed Penuel, limping because of his hip.

Genesis 32:24-31

The creation of woman is the result of a deliberate decision by Lord God, not an afterthought. The Lord God wants to make man 'a helper as his partner'. We again hear this repetition in 2:20, 'but for the man there was not found a helper as his partner'. Yet, when woman is created, the man names her neither helper nor partner, but elevates her status to, 'bone of my bones and flesh of my flesh' (2:23).

The movement of the story in Genesis 2 is that Lord God keeps improving on creation.

- At first, there is no plant or greenery of the field (2:5), so Lord God creates a garden (2:8)
- When there is no rain to water the garden (2:5), Lord God causes a stream to rise from the earth (2:5)
- Needing someone to till the ground (2:5) Lord God fashions a human being (2:7)
- And when the human being needs a companion (2:18), Lord God creates woman (2:22-23)

Lord God takes a rib from man (2:21), taken from his side, for the person created is to be beside him and wrapped around his heart. So meticulous in its description. The working hands of Lord God operating, working, creating and tenderly touching, knowing every detail, entering into every intricacy of our lives.

> [13] For it was you who formed my inward parts;
> you knit me together in my mother's womb.
> [14] I praise you, for I am fearfully and wonderfully made.
> Wonderful are your works;
> that I know very well.
> [15] My frame was not hidden from you,
> when I was being made in secret,
> intricately woven in the depths of the earth.
>
> Psalm 139:13-15

The Lord God creates in a way that gifts us and all living creatures with the ability to continue to beget new life, to give birth to 'flesh of our flesh' (2:23). We can co-create out of our own willingness. And what is born is ours to love and name our own. However, today there are other means of begetting.

The author of the Genesis creation account did not broach such issues as surrogacy or IVF, but what is fundamentally clear here is that what is formed is done so out of a desire for love and what is born is brought into a relationship of love. It is to share flesh! What is not acceptable is:

- Creating life in order to abuse it
- To beget life without acknowledging the partner
- Without love or respect for the other
- To abort
- To disown or neglect
- To reduce to mechanical means
- To manipulate life form

If there is a mystery at the heart of the human condition, it is otherness: the otherness of woman and man, parent and child as Rabbi Jonathan Sacks notes. It is the space we make for the otherness that makes love something other than narcissism, and parenthood something greater than self-replication. We are each in God's image but no one else's.[58]

> **Genesis 2:23** *Then the man said,*
> *'This at last is bone of my bones*
> *and flesh of my flesh;*
> *this one shall be called Woman,*
> *for out of Man this one was taken'.*

The Lord God creates us to fall head over heels in love with another and deliberately does so for our good, 'It is not good that man should be alone; I will make him a helper as his partner' (2:18). In the intimacy of relationship, people are drawn to one another and to God. This is the ultimate experience of love.

In both creation accounts, the climax is the creation of human beings and the understanding of equality 'bone of my bones and flesh of my flesh'.

Barbara E. Reid elaborates that 'helper' in Hebrew is *ezer*, but astonishingly, *ezer* is masculine in gender, even though it refers to the woman. More amazingly, the word *ezer* is often used to refer to YHWH in relation to Israel. YHWH is

---

[58] Rabbi Jonathan Sacks, *Covenant and Conversation: A weekly reading of the Jewish Bible. Genesis: The Book of Beginnings*, (New Milford, USA: Maggid Books, 2009), 151.

Israel's *ezer*, Israel's 'strong deliverer', 'mighty companion,' 'saver.'[59] The woman saved man from his isolation. She was his *ezer* – his 'deliverer', his 'companion', his 'saver'.

To be a helper is to possess the knowledge and skills to assist and further the other's plans. To ask for help from another is to rely on them and trust they can offer needed assistance. To help is to support one another and build up one another.

To be a partner is to be by the side of another, the one that completes me. To be a partner is to willingly go where the other goes and to share the journey and divide the riches!

Bone of my bones and flesh of my flesh is the most intimate of relationships. To be so much involved and part of the other, that life finds its meaning only with the other. That whatever grieves or hurts me, hurts the other. Whatever gives joy to me, so too the other. It is as if the two have become so entwined they are one person.

The man sees the woman as a mirror of himself, one intimately bound to him. Woman and man, born to realise the full potential of one another, to fulfil hopes and participate in ongoing creation. There is desire, intimacy, union and love shared. Nothing less is expected by God or from either of them. Woman and man share responsibilities and have each other for support in life.

'This at last.' What a relief! We spend our years searching for that one person whom we can draw close to, the one we dare to open ourselves to and welcome in our lives and then ah! What a relief! The man recognises this woman before

---

[59] Barbara E. Reid, *Wisdom's Feast. An Invitation to Feminist Interpretation of the Scriptures*, (Grand Rapids, Michigan: William B. Eerdmans Publishing Company, 2016), 19.

him as someone of his equal, someone he can respect and spend his life with.

> I give you a new commandment, that you love one another. Just as I have loved you, you also should love one another.
>
> John 13:34 (and John 15:12-13)

Partnership is precious and willingly entered into on both sides for the purpose of fulfilment emotionally, socially, physically and importantly, spiritually.

> **Genesis 2:24-25** *Therefore a man leaves his father and his mother and clings to his wife, and they become one flesh. ²⁵ And the man and his wife were both naked, and were not ashamed.*

The primary meaning of two becoming one flesh is not male-female sexual union, but two people forming a new family. The word flesh in the Bible almost always refers to a kinship bind.

> Laban said to him, 'Surely you are my bone and my flesh!' And he stayed with him for a month.
>
> Genesis 29:14
> (also see Judges 9:2 and 2 Samuel 19:12)

According to Richard Hess, to fully appreciate the intended unity of male and female, it is important to notice the materials employed in their creation. The man comes from the ground. In Hebrew, the most common means of expressing the feminine gender is with a suffix *-ah*. The word for 'man' in most of chapter two is *'adam*. The ground from which the man is created in 2:7 is *'adamah*. Therefore, when God introduces the woman to the man, he cannot use the *'adam/'adamah* distinction. Instead, the man uses two new words, *'ishah* for woman, and *'ish* for man. Thus, as the man (*'adam*) was taken from the ground (*'adamah*) and will return to it (3:19), so the woman (*'ishah*) was taken from the man (*'ish*). However, instead of the woman returning to the man, the man returns to the woman (2:24). The man and woman together create 'one flesh'. This reverses the expected means of reconnection and so avoids any sense that the woman is a derivative secondary figure who must find her way back to the man for completion. This symmetry of activity emphasises harmony rather than dependence, as noted that the woman and man were naked and unashamed (2:25).[60]

We need to forge our own life and that often includes a hoped-for, long-term relationship, or as the Bible passage describes it, 'clings to his wife' (2:24). This strong image could be interpreted as dependent or possessive of the other. Or it could suggest a cleaving away from something else in order to cling to another. It is emotional effort, tearing from the hold of parents/other, and running into the arms of another. Hearts are broken, hearts are captured.

Just as we cling to one another, so too do we of God, just as God clings to us (Deuteronomy 4:4, 10:20, 11:22, 13:4, 30:20, 31:6; Joshua 22:5, 23:8; 1 Kings 6:13; 2 Kings 18:6; Jeremiah 13:11; Psalm 119:31)

---

[60] Richard Hess, 'Evidence for Equality in Genesis 1-3,' in *Christians for Biblical Equality International*, Autumn 2008, Vol 7, Issue 3, p. 9.

The rendering in Genesis 2:24 as 'leaves', is a relatively pale rendering according to Megan Warner. The Hebrew verb is generally understood as the man 'abandons' his parents. Yet the 'abandoning' of one's parents is not generally something encouraged in the Hebrew Scriptures. On the contrary, one of their foundational directives is the injunction to 'honour' one's father and one's mother (Exodus 20:12; Deuteronomy 5:16). In the face of this commandment, the description in Genesis 2:24 of 'abandoning' parents is surprising.[61]

Although Genesis 2:24 presents an etiology, it is not a normative etiology of marriage but a descriptive etiology of the strong draw and attraction that calls women and men into relationship with one another. Genesis 2:24 acknowledges the propensity of men to pursue 'inappropriate' marriages, particularly intermarriages, that defy the wishes and schemes of their parents and, by implication, society and religious institutions (Joshua 23:12, Exodus 34:11-16 and Deuteronomy 7:1-6). It is in Genesis 2:24 that we come to understand the power of the need for relationship.[62]

Relationships can hurt, and they can captivate and take hold of us. Relationships take effort and determination, but they matter most for our functioning.

> In the Bible, the man-woman couple is not meant to be simply a means for preservation of the species, as is the case for the other animals. Insofar as it was called to become the image and likeness of God, it

---

[61] Megan Warner, "Therefore a Man Leaves His Father and His Mother and Clings to His Wife": Marriage and Intermarriage in Genesis 2:24 in *Journal of Biblical Literature*, Vol. 136, No. 2 (Summer 2017), 276.

[62] Warner, "Therefore a Man Leaves His Father and His Mother and Clings to His Wife": Marriage and Intermarriage in Genesis 2:24, p. 288.

expresses in a bodily, tangible way the face of God, which is Love. We could say that sexual otherness forces men and women to be like God, in the sense of having to place themselves in a relationship of sympathy, of synergy, of communion, of fruitfulness. From this fact arises the Christian's profound respect for the body and for sexuality, whose dignity must never be distorted or sold short. Hence, sexuality can be neither 'unruly' nor 'unreasonable': it has a meaning, a direction, rules and boundaries... For I exist only if I am loved, and I exist only if I love. Truly, love is that divine element that allows our body to exist.

Carlo Maria Martini[63]

In my nakedness, I am exposed and vulnerable. Others can take advantage of that for their own lustful satisfaction but in a true relationship the giving of our bare-naked selves is freely bestowed and passionately given. It is the total, abandoned generous giving of all I am to the one who is all of me.

On this note of human encounter and love, let us pause and take an overall look at God creating. In the first Creation account, we see God doing the following:

- God created (1:1, 21, 27)
- Wind from God swept (1:2)
- God said (1:3, 6, 9, 11, 14, 20, 24, 26, 28, 29)
- God saw (1:4, 10, 12, 18, 21, 25, 31)
- God separated (1:4)
- God called (1:8, 10)

---

[63] Carlo Maria Martini, *On the Body. A Contemporary Theology of the Human Person*, (Victoria: John Garratt Publishing, 2000), 44.

- God made (1:7, 16, 25)
- God set them (1:17)
- God blessed (1:22, 28, 2:3)
- God finished and rested (2:2-3)

In the second account of Creation, we see the Lord God do the following:

- Made (2:4)
- Formed (2:7, 19)
- Breathed (2:7)
- Planted (2:7)
- Put (2:7)
- Made to grow (2:9)
- Took (2:15, 21-22)
- Commanded (2:16)
- Said (2:18)
- Brought (2:19, 22)
- Caused (2:21)

In the first creation account, it is a God who speaks and observes and thus creates. In the second account, the Lord God is more hands on, intimate with the happenings of creation, plotting and planning, changing and creating. It is a work in progress.

The similarity in both accounts is that creation is not a sudden appearance, a BIG BANG, and there it was! It is a long, thoughtful process over time. Creation develops after thought. It begets new things in the process. Life moves forward and changes and adapts to new ways of being.

To summarise the creation accounts, we can highlight the following:

- the equality of the sexes
- mutual complementarity between woman and man
- affording each other companionship
- the gift and responsibility of creative, fruitful love
- the person is a moral subject capable of self-direction and self-determination through the exercise of freedom
- the person is called to stewardship, to responsibility to care for life and be co-creators with the Lord God.

That draws to a close the creation texts. Two different by complimentary versions. We are now left to contemplate how humans survive in this new paradise. So, let us continue the journey through the Book of Genesis.

Chapter 7

Despite troubles

The third chapter of the Book of Genesis narrows its gaze to the woman and man in the garden and a very crafty serpent!

> Now the serpent was more crafty than any other wild animal that the LORD God had made. He said to the woman, 'Did God say, "You shall not eat from any tree in the garden"?' ²The woman said to the serpent, 'We may eat of the fruit of the trees in the garden; ³but God said, "You shall not eat of the fruit of the tree that is in the middle of the garden, nor shall you touch it, or you shall die." ' ⁴But the serpent said to the woman, 'You will not die; ⁵for God knows that when you eat of it your eyes will be opened, and you will be like God, knowing good and evil.' ⁶So when the woman saw that the tree was good for food, and that it was a delight to the eyes, and that the tree was to be desired to make one wise, she took of its fruit and ate; and she also gave some to her husband, who was with her, and he ate.
> ⁷Then the eyes of both were opened, and they knew that they were naked; and they sewed fig leaves together and made loincloths for themselves.
> ⁸They heard the sound of the LORD God walking in the garden at the time of the evening breeze, and the man and his wife hid themselves from the presence of the LORD God among the trees of the garden. ⁹But the LORD God called

to the man, and said to him, 'Where are you?' ¹⁰He said, 'I heard the sound of you in the garden, and I was afraid, because I was naked; and I hid myself.' ¹¹He said, 'Who told you that you were naked? Have you eaten from the tree of which I commanded you not to eat?' ¹²The man said, 'The woman whom you gave to be with me, she gave me fruit from the tree, and I ate.' ¹³Then the LORD God said to the woman, 'What is this that you have done?' The woman said, 'The serpent tricked me, and I ate.' ¹⁴The LORD God said to the serpent,

> 'Because you have done this,
>   cursed are you among all animals
>   and among all wild creatures;
> upon your belly you shall go,
>   and dust you shall eat
>   all the days of your life.
> ¹⁵I will put enmity between you and the woman,
>   and between your offspring and hers;
> he will strike your head,
>   and you will strike his heel.'

¹⁶To the woman he said,

> 'I will greatly increase your pangs in childbearing;
>   in pain you shall bring forth children,
> yet your desire shall be for your husband,
>   and he shall rule over you.'

¹⁷And to the man he said,

> 'Because you have listened to the voice of your wife,
>   and have eaten of the tree

> about which I commanded you,
>   "You shall not eat of it",
> cursed is the ground because of you;
>   in toil you shall eat of it all the days of your life;
> [18]thorns and thistles it shall bring forth for you;
>   and you shall eat the plants of the field.
> [19]By the sweat of your face
>   you shall eat bread
> until you return to the ground,
>   for out of it you were taken;
> you are dust,
>   and to dust you shall return.'

[20]The man named his wife Eve, because she was the mother of all who live. [21]And the LORD God made garments of skins for the man and for his wife, and clothed them. [22]Then the LORD God said, 'See, the man has become like one of us, knowing good and evil; and now, he might reach out his hand and take also from the tree of life, and eat, and live for ever'— [23]therefore the LORD God sent him forth from the garden of Eden, to till the ground from which he was taken. [24]He drove out the man; and at the east of the garden of Eden he placed the cherubim, and a sword flaming and turning to guard the way to the tree of life.

Genesis 3:1-24

The Book of Genesis is Israel's answer to the problem of evil, by stating that there is only one God, that creation is good, that humans are made in God's image and evil is not outside but within us.

Genesis 3:1 *Now the serpent was more crafty than any other wild animal that the* LORD *God had made.*

The snake and the tree of life are traditional elements in many mythological stories of origins.

- The hero in the Babylonian epic Gilgamesh, having been given a shoot from a plant that will rejuvenate him, loses it to a snake, who swallows it.
- In the Mesopotamian legend of Adapa, the first man is allowed into the council of the gods, who offer him the bread and water of life, which would give him immortality and divine status. He thinks this a trick, so refuses, forfeiting his chance to be with the gods.
- The serpent was a recognised symbol of fertility cults, a 'fertilising phallus,' and a seductive temptation to the people of Israel. That is why the serpent is introduced as the woman's companion and not the man's in the Genesis account.

Genesis 3 brings together these mythical elements, as the serpent tempts the first couple to grasp at immortality and wisdom. The use of the serpent, combined with temptation, the manner of awareness and shame of their nakedness, portrays the message that the fertility cults cause unease.[64]

---

[64] David James Stewart, 'The emergence of consciousness in Genesis 1–3: Jung's depth psychology and theological anthropology,' in *Zygon*, vol. 49, no. 2 (June 2014), p. 523.

The serpent is more *arum* than any other wild animal. The meaning of the word in Hebrew is ambiguous. It is sometimes used negatively as crafty or shrewd.

> He frustrates the devices of the crafty, so that their hands achieve no success.
>
> Job 5:12 (and Job 15:5)

But more often in the wisdom literature, it is used positively meaning sensible or prudent (Proverbs 14:15; 22:3; 27:12).

The craftiness of the serpent is only as poisonous as we allow it to be. Otherwise it slithers back to its dark abode. And yet, the serpent appears to possess practical wisdom, as do other wild animals.

> For in vain is the net baited while the bird is looking on.
>
> Proverbs 1:17

The Lord God is attributed the creating of the serpent which is described as 'crafty'. Is this suggesting the Lord God too is 'crafty?' Furthermore, the Lord God has created other wild animals. The description provided suggests God is not tame. The Lord God creates but there is in creating, factors characterising boldness, wildness, cunning, power, difference, danger. In the Book of Job, God takes responsibility for creating the wild creatures.

¹⁵'Look at Behemoth, which I made just as I made you; it eats grass like an ox. ¹⁶Its strength is in its loins, and its power in the muscles of its belly. ¹⁷It makes its tail stiff like a cedar; the sinews of its thighs are knit together. ¹⁸Its bones are tubes of bronze, its limbs like bars of iron.'

Job 40:15-18 (and 41:1-2)

In the garden of Eden, that paradise place, the woman and man encounter the crafty serpent. The Lord God creates a world that is beautiful but at the same time it has elements that are crafty and wild. The world is a place of fear and awe, magnificent boldness, deceptional beauty and humans are in the midst of it. The challenge is to know how to live with seduction and temptation.

Genesis 3:1 *He said to the woman, 'Did God say, "You shall not eat from any tree in the garden"?'*

The serpent enters into conversation with the woman. Evil is not depicted as one with weapons, waging war, who is dark, ugly, and brutal. Evil is much more subtle and closer to us than we know. It keeps to the fringes or hides in the background, always watching carefully. Evil creeps in unaware and sows discord, planting doubt and suspicion, it manipulates words into tempting lies. It hints at deceit, but all the while plays the 'innocent' one. It leads us to question the goodness around us and leaves us unsatisfied with ourselves, others and with God.

The personification of the serpent creates a twist in that the gift of words, which separates humans from animals, is here used against humans.

> And the LORD God *commanded* the man, 'You may *freely eat* of every tree of the garden'.
>
> Genesis 2:16
>
> He said to the woman, 'Did God say, "You *shall not eat* from any tree in the garden"?'
>
> Genesis 3:1

The serpent jumbles and rearranges the Lord God's words. The Lord God did not 'say' (3:1), but instead 'commanded' (2:16). The serpent reverses what the Lord God had said, for God's words had pronounced freedom, not limitation. The serpent uses half-truths, avoiding mentioning the Lord God's generosity, instead focusing on the one prohibition, which the serpent subtly suggests is unreasonably harsh.

Although the serpent never directly tells the woman to transgress the Lord God's commandment, by playing with words, the serpent calls into question both the truthfulness (by denying the warning) and trustworthiness (by impugning the motives) of the Lord God, leaving the woman to draw her own conclusions. The only power that evil has is through human belief in its lies, achieved through manipulation of words.

The fact that the serpent undermines God's trustworthiness and truthfulness, leaving the woman to draw her own conclusions, points to the real core of human alienation from God and the real root of disobedience. It is not that God and humans can no longer converse, explains R. W. L. Moberly, but rather the difficulty is that the human heart and mind can have in genuinely trusting God as a wise creator and live accordingly.[65]

With the power of words, the serpent uses the term 'Elohim' rather than 'Yahweh Elohim', which is used in the surrounding narrative, except again in the woman's response, which echoes the serpent. This changing of title is a subtle way of displaying one's disrespect.

And the LORD *God* - Genesis 2:16

He said to the woman, 'Did *God*...' - Genesis 3:1

The woman said to the serpent, '... but *God* said' – Genesis 3:2-3

How we view the other determines how we interpret their words. If we hold them in high esteem, we pay close attention to what they have to say and we keep an open mind. On the other hand, if we live in fear or dislike of the person, we distort their words.

Whose voice is heard and whose voice matters? Is it the one that gets into our ear? What are our encounters with others like? Fickle, deceitful or harmful? Are our relationships serpentine – smooth talking with malicious intent? The message to be learnt is that only the Lord God's words hold true and are the voice of reason.

In the account, the serpent approaches the woman by pretending to be her friend, concerned only for her welfare,

---

[65] Moberly, R. W. L. 'Genesis 2–3: Adam and Eve and "the Fall"' in *The Theology of the Book of Genesis*. (Cambridge Books Online, Cambridge University Press, 2009), 86.

and begins by saying something only partly true, 'Did God really say you were not to eat from any of the trees in the garden?' (Genesis 3:1). In fact, the Lord God never told the man not to eat from any tree, but only from the one tree, 'Of the tree of the knowledge of good and evil you are not to eat' (Genesis 2:17).

The serpent represents people of today who poke fun at God, deliberately misinterpret God's words, mocking and subverting God's message. They will ask questions but do not seek an answer. And people today who listen to lies, as a result, turn their back on God, whom they deduce is deceitful. So, we choose a world without God, but is there such a place? We persist with our stubborn denial of the divine, of goodness, of harmony. In denying God, we deny the created world as it is and so we create or understand it in another way – shallow, empty, transient. A world without God becomes a world of I and too many egos begin to threaten one another. We quickly forget that God space gives us breathing space to rest and be loved. And we soon discover that human space is constantly a struggle to survive.

> **Genesis 3:2-3** *The woman said to the serpent, 'We may eat of the fruit of the trees in the garden; but God said, "You shall not eat of the fruit of the tree that is in the middle of the garden, nor shall you touch it, or you shall die."'*

The woman was approached because she had not heard the decree the Lord God had commanded the man in Genesis 2:16-17. So, let us compare the two, the words of the Lord God to the man, and the woman's interpretation of the words said to her by the man.

God (Genesis 2:16-17)	**Woman (Genesis 3:2-3)**
1. And the LORD God commanded the man	but God said
2. You may freely eat	We may eat
3. of every tree of the garden;	of the fruit of the trees in the garden;
4. but of the tree of the knowledge of good and evil	the fruit of the tree that is in the middle of the garden,
5. you shall not eat	you shall not eat
6. for in the day that you eat of it you shall die.	nor shall you touch it, or you shall die

There are quite a lot of inconsistencies between the two passages so let us compare and examine the statements.

1. The first is weakening of the Lord God's words. The Lord God had commanded, not said. The message given was meant to be understood clearly, so that excuses would not be permitted.

2. The verb 'We may eat', lacks the emphasis of God's initial word.

> 2:16 The Lord God commanded - *You may freely eat*
> 3:1 The serpent said - *Did God say, "You shall not eat...*
> 3:2 The woman claims God said - *We may eat...*

One statement, but three very different claims. So how do they differ? The statement was positive, 'You may freely eat'. It was framed as a welcoming invitation to come and be satisfied. The woman interpreted this part correctly because it appealed to her. The serpent got it very wrong, rewording the claim to announce, 'You shall not eat.' A dark and negative interpretation, typical of evil intents.

3. The Lord God said to 'eat of every tree'. The woman generalises, 'eat of the fruit of the trees', reducing the claim of generosity given by the Lord God. The serpent says, 'not eat from any tree' in total contrast to the original command. The serpent changes the intention and sentiment of the Lord God's words. The serpent tells a deliberate and manipulative lie.

4. The Lord God created 'the tree of life also in the midst of the garden' (2:9). However, when the Lord God commanded the man, there was only reference to every tree and the tree of knowledge of good and evil.

> **Genesis 2:16-17** And the LORD God commanded the man, 'You may freely eat of every tree of the garden but of the tree of the knowledge of good and evil you shall not eat, for in the day that you eat of it you shall die'.

Yet when the woman is questioned by the serpent, she does not refer to the tree of knowledge of good and evil. She instead states, 'You shall not eat of the fruit of the tree that is in the middle of the garden'. The tree in the middle of the garden is the tree of life and the LORD God made no mention of this tree when the man was commanded.

5. If we continue, we note the following:

> 2:17 Lord God goes on to say - *but of the tree of the knowledge of good and evil you shall not eat, for in the day that you eat of it you shall die.*
>
> 3:3 And the woman makes the statement - *but God said, "You shall not eat of the fruit of the tree that is in the middle of the garden, nor shall you touch it, or you shall die."*

Death comes from eating of the tree of knowledge of good and evil, not the tree of life which was in the middle of the garden. Yet the serpent never mentions any of this in its original words. The serpent let the woman take the bait. He planted the seed of doubt in her mind. The serpent gave her enough rope basically to hang herself!

6. The woman increases the scope of the Lord God's prohibition by adding, 'nor shall you touch it'. It is not difficult to see in the woman's answers, some uncertainty and lack of confidence in what the Lord God said – hence her saying both less and more. The woman makes no reference to what the tree can offer. All she knows about the tree is that if you touch it, 'you shall die' (3:3). Yet Lord God had told the man, 'in the day that you eat of it you shall die' (2:17). It is the serpent who tells the woman that it leads to 'knowing good and evil' (3:5).

The woman's original understanding is limited and somewhat childlike. It is what we tell children, 'Do not touch this or you will be in trouble', and we point to whatever object we are referring to. The woman too can only identify the tree as 'in the middle of the garden'. Such knowledge proves insufficient when the woman was challenged by the serpent. When it offered her more information about the tree, the woman's curiosity was heightened. So, is the woman to blame if she originally had not been correctly informed of the state of affairs? It seems this has been the approach taken as we read in Sirach 25:24, 'From a woman sin had its beginning, and because of her we all die'.

Why did the Lord God not reveal the fuller truth to the woman when the Lord God spoke to the man? And why did the man not tell the full truth to the woman as relayed to him by the Lord God?

- Was he afraid the woman would know too much?
- Did he assume the woman would not understand?
- Was he afraid that the woman might be tempted?
- Did the man think that the woman did not need to know about good and evil?
- Did the man barely take notice of what the Lord God said and so only relayed minimal information to the woman?
- Did he hold back information in an attempt to keep the woman submissive?
- Did he withhold information so as not to expose her to the harsh reality of life?

Whatever the reason, the woman should have been given the full picture. This would have saved them all heartache. Withholding information leads to misunderstanding. Trust is lost. When we deny knowledge to others, they will get it in other ways, through other means, and it may become misconstrued. We need to trust that what we know is important and passing on our knowledge to others allows them to be better informed and so make discerned decisions. When we are treated as a child, we will behave as such. When we are treated as mature, knowledgeable adults, we take on more responsibility for our words, choices and actions. Unfortunately, the serpent slithered its way into the heart and sight of the woman and slyly fed her its own propaganda and conspiracy theories.

> **Genesis 3:4-5** *But the serpent said to the woman, 'You will not die; ⁵for God knows that when you eat of it your eyes will be opened, and you will be like God, knowing good and evil.'*

So, who is telling the truth in this myth? Most people assume that the Lord God is right and the serpent is lying. But the serpent does not seem to be lying.

- The serpent says: 'Your eyes will be opened' (3:5). Their eyes are opened (3:7).
- The serpent says: 'You will be like God, knowing good and evil' (3:5). They become like God, knowing good and evil (3:22).
- The Lord God had said: 'In the day that you eat of it you shall die' (2:17). The serpent says: 'You will not die' (3:4). They ate and did not die.

Careful analysis reveals the serpent 'gets wrong' what the Lord God had originally said, inverting permission into prohibition (3:1). Yet, there is an innuendo, in such inversion, to the effect that one might more naturally associate the Lord God with restriction rather than generosity. As Moberly explains, such a tacit implication about God's character is not necessarily dismissed by pointing out the obvious inaccuracy of the serpent's words.[66]

Many theologians and philosophers consider moral reasoning an essential element of what it means to be human. This moral reasoning is implied in the knowledge humans gain from the tree. If this knowledge is essential to being human, then, we can argue, the serpent plays a central and essential role.[67] Perhaps the serpent is not so evil after all!

The biblical account has the serpent beguile the woman into eating the fruit. The serpent's suggestion in the garden and the devil's in the desert are both very reasonable.

> Then Jesus was led up by the Spirit into the wilderness to be tempted by the devil. ²He fasted for forty days and forty nights, and afterwards he was famished. ³The tempter came and said to him, 'If you are the Son of God, command these stones to become loaves of bread.' ⁴But he answered, 'It is written,

---

[66] Moberly, R. W. L. 'Genesis 2–3: Adam and Eve and "the Fall"' in *The Theology of the Book of Genesis*. (Cambridge Books Online, Cambridge University Press, 2009), 79.

[67] Arthur Walker-Jones, 'Naming the human animal: Genesis 1-3 and other animals in human becoming' in *Zygon*, Vol 52, no. 4, (December 2017), 1023.

"One does not live by bread alone,
but by every word that comes from the mouth of God."'
⁵Then the devil took him to the holy city and placed him on the pinnacle of the temple, ⁶saying to him, 'If you are the Son of God, throw yourself down; for it is written,
"He will command his angels concerning you",
and "On their hands they will bear you up,
so that you will not dash your foot against a stone."'
⁷Jesus said to him, 'Again it is written, "Do not put the Lord your God to the test."'
⁸Again, the devil took him to a very high mountain and showed him all the kingdoms of the world and their splendour; ⁹and he said to him, 'All these I will give you, if you will fall down and worship me.'
¹⁰Jesus said to him, 'Away with you, Satan! for it is written,
"Worship the Lord your God,
and serve only him."'
¹¹Then the devil left him, and suddenly angels came and waited on him.

Matthew 4:1-11

Jesus' earthly ministry is framed by invitations to use for his own purposes God's power that he has as Son of God (Matthew 4:1–11). First, to turn stone into bread so as to meet his hunger; second, to claim God's promise of protection as specified in Scripture; third, through a compromise, to claim a dominion that is already promised to him. At the end (Matthew 27:38–44), as Jesus hangs dying on the cross, the same, 'If you are the Son of God' recurs, now with a proposal that he should come down from the cross so that Israel's leaders would believe in him. As R. W. L. Moberly explains, no great transgression of God's moral will would be involved, nothing very weighty might appear to be at stake, such that one could hardly find fault with Jesus for going along with the suggestions put to him. And yet, what it means for Jesus to be Son of God, in which his refusal to go along with the enticing suggestions, is not marginal but fundamental to the whole meaning of his trusting and obedient sonship.[68]

As Gerard W. Hughes also notes, why not accept what looks good and promises power, and why not turn stone into bread to satisfy our own and other people's hunger? Why are the temptations portrayed in this way so subtle and so reasonable? Because the nature of evil is that it creeps on us like a serpent and appears to be good and reasonable. However, if we pursue any of these good things at the expense of others, then the good we pursue becomes destructive, to ourselves and others.[69]

The experience of stepping outside the realm of obedient trust in the Lord God can often appear positive, as it did for the woman. It looks attractive on its own terms, and the immediate result can be a sense of enlargement and liberation ('eyes opened'). It is, therefore, often the case that, in the terms of the narrative, apparently the Lord God is wrong, and the serpent is right.[70] Yet as R. W. L. Moberly elaborates, the context of puzzlement

---
[68] Moberly, 'Genesis 2–3: Adam and Eve and "the Fall"', 82-83.
[69] Gerard W Hughes, *God of Surprises*, (London: Darton, Longman and Todd Ltd, 2003).
[70] Moberly, 'Genesis 2–3: Adam and Eve and "the Fall"', 85.

and disillusionment may also be the context of moral and spiritual maturing. For one may look again at principles already held and dig deeper, to ask whether they may indeed be true even if such truth is no longer at a surface level. This is the strategy employed within Genesis 2–3, to lead into a deeper understanding of what is meant by 'death' as the consequence of disobedience to God. The felt liberation may be misleading, for death may be present metaphorically as a diminution of, and alienation within, the personal and the public life of humanity.[71] Or as Pope Francis writes:

> The tempter's 'deconstruction' then takes on an appearance of truth: 'God knows that on the day you eat it your eyes will be opened and you will be like gods, knowing good and evil' (*Gen 3:5*). God's paternal command, meant for their good, is discredited by the seductive enticement of the enemy: 'The woman saw that the tree was good to eat and pleasing to the eye and desirable' (*Genesis 3:6*)...
> The economic and manipulative aims that feed disinformation are rooted in a thirst for power, a desire to possess and enjoy, which ultimately makes us victims of something much more tragic: the deceptive power of evil that moves from one lie to another in order to rob us of our interior freedom. That is why education for truth means teaching people how to discern, evaluate and understand our deepest desires and inclinations, lest we lose sight of what is good and yield to every temptation.[72]

---

[71] Moberly, 'Genesis 2–3: Adam and Eve and "the Fall"', 86.
[72] Pope Francis, LII World Communications Day, 2018 http://www.vatican.va/content/francesco/en/messages/communications/documents/papa-francesco_20180124_messaggio-comunicazioni-sociali.html

People find themselves at the crossroads where they say, 'If I obey God I'll miss out! I need to be happy'. That is the justification. Sin always begins with the 'character assassination of God' as Timothy Keller puts it. We believe that God has put us in a world of delights but will not give them to us if we obey him. This is the lie of the serpent, the original temptation of humans.[73]

'To be like God, knowing good and evil.' To be God is to be someone who has perfect discernment. The difference between what is good and what is evil is not as clear cut as assumed but requires a person to be neither influenced by the clattering of propaganda, nor swayed by lies. Yet can one be totally free of bias in judgment of good or evil, right or wrong?

If we want to 'be like God, knowing good and evil', then we also need to be responsible for our choices and the consequences that follow. To be Godlike is not to yield power and have insurpassable knowledge, but to assess each moment, to take responsibility for making the best possible choices. God-becoming is no joyride. God's choices must be life-giving in every possible way, otherwise all of us will fall, for God's choices impact us all. So, to be like God is perseverance to choose good from evil, each and every time.

Yet are we not at times like the trickster serpent! So quick to play the devil's advocate, to discredit another, to manipulate words, to be a spin doctor. We cause division, arouse false assumptions, encourage doubt, question motives,

---

[73] Timothy Keller, *The Prodigal Prophet. Jonah and the mystery of God's mercy*, (Great Britain: Hodder & Stoughton, 2018), 138.

instigate suspicion, put a wedge in relationships, dishonour goodness, silence truth, deny justice and prevent righteousness. We cast the bait and reel them in.

So how do we avoid being reeled in and trapped by lies and half-truths or prevent ourselves from instigating the reeling in? It is to keep God ever before us or else the serpent will slither in. To take words at face value is risky, as there is always more we should know.

> **Genesis 3:6** *So when the woman saw that the tree was good for food, and that it was a delight to the eyes, and that the tree was to be desired to make one wise, she took of its fruit and ate; and she also gave some to her husband, who was with her, and he ate.*

The story has the woman see that the tree is 'good for food', 'a delight to the eyes' and 'to be desired to make one wise'. She can see nothing wrong, only something attractive and promising, concerning nourishment, beauty and insight. The motivation in taking the fruit is a mixture of physical attraction and curiosity. The woman is, therefore, depicted as observing, reflecting before she eats, active and knowledgeable. The man on the other hand is silent, passive and acquiescent.

The woman 'saw the tree was good'. Let us pause here and cast our minds back to the beginning. Can we see the connection? God too saw that it was good. What we have here is a behaviour by the woman that reflects that of God – the ability to see and to recognise and appreciate what is around us. The verse continues with the woman recognising 'it was a delight to the eyes'. The beauty of life dazzles one. The problem, however, lies in how far we become enamoured with life.

Comparing Genesis 2:8-9 with Genesis 3:6, there are similarities but also differences that reveal a great deal between the Lord God and humans.

> **Genesis 2:8-9** And the LORD God planted a garden in Eden, in the east; and there he put the man whom he had formed. ⁹Out of the ground the LORD God made to grow every tree that is pleasant to the sight and good for food, the tree of life also in the midst of the garden, and the tree of the knowledge of good and evil.

> **Genesis 3:6** So when the woman saw that the tree was good for food, and that it was a delight to the eyes, and that the tree was to be desired to make one wise, she took of its fruit and ate; and she also gave some to her husband, who was with her, and he ate.

The Lord God placed man in the garden, with the tree of life and tree of knowledge of good and evil. The Lord God notices that every tree is pleasant to the sight and then that it is good for food.

The woman only focuses on the one tree, that it was good for food, that it was a delight to the eyes and desired to make one wise. The woman delights and desires. She eats and shares with the man. Humans yearn and crave for what is good and pleasant.

God saw it was good and stopped there. God allows creation to be, just as it is. God appreciates the intrinsic value of each thing. We humans, on the other hand, are enamoured by the splendour around us, and cannot let things be. We delight in it but we also desire it for our benefit, 'the tree was to be desired to make one wise' (3:6). We place our wants first and measure the goodness of everything according to how it benefits us. We cannot simply let them 'be'. Rather they must 'be' for our purposes. This unsatisfied desire is also told in the Greek myth that describes humans and the troubles that befall them.

> Another of Zeus' sons created a woman of great beauty, Pandora. Each of the gods gave her a gift. Zeus' present was curiosity and a box which he ordered her never to open. Then he presented her to Epimetheus as a wife.
>
> Pandora's life with Epimetheus was happy except for her intense longing to open the box. She was convinced that because the gods and goddesses had showered so many glorious gifts upon her that this one would also be wonderful. One day when Epimetheus was gone she opened the box.
>
> Out of the box flew all of the horrors which plague the world today – pain, sickness, envy, greed. Upon hearing Pandora's screams, Epimetheus rushed home and fastened the lid shut, but all of the evils had already escaped.
>
> Later that night they heard a voice coming from the box saying, 'Let me out. I am hope'.
>
> Pandora and Epimetheus released her and she flew out into the world to give hope to humankind.
>
> https://www.cs.williams.edu/~lindsey/myths/myths_16.html

Julien C. H. Smith and T. Laine Scales warn us that the aspirations of Prometheus, as well as the behaviour of the woman and man, offer a cautionary tale. In principle, everything cannot be mastered. To do so is to think of ourselves as other than we are: as masters of what we possess by right, rather than stewards of what we are graciously entrusted with.[74]

Both the woman and the man eat of the fruit. The woman because she saw its benefits. The man ate for any of the following reasons:

- Simply because he followed what the woman did
- He was hungry
- He was desirous of wisdom

The text does not claim a moment of reflection on the part of the man. There is no hint of the man's resistance or hesitation, and no words issue forth from him. Therefore, the conclusion that the woman is a temptress is not substantiated. In fact, the serpent in speaking to the woman had used the plural form, suggesting the man was within earshot. The woman had given it to her husband who was 'with her' (3:12).[75]

The possibility of the man's presence during the serpent-woman dialogue is the woman's use of the first-person plural (we may eat) in 3:2b. Yet, the man is never directly mentioned, addressed, consulted, or acknowledged in

---

[74] Julien C. H. Smith and T. Laine Scales, 'Stewardship: A Biblical Model for the Formation of Christian Scholars,' in *JECB* 17:1 (2013), 90.

[75] Dumbrell, *Covenant and Creation. An Old Testament Covenant Theology*, 50.

any way until the woman gives him the fruit in 3:6b.[76] Translations that fail to convey that the man is 'with her' enables readers to excuse the man and condemn the woman as Julie Faith Parker asserts. Blaming the woman alone brings considerable consequences not only for understanding Genesis 3:6, but also for generating ideas about women.[77]

> You are the one who opened the door to the Devil. You are the one who first plucked the fruit of the forbidden tree, you are the first who deserted the divine law; you are the one who persuaded him whom the Devil was not strong enough to attack. All too easily you destroyed the image of God, namely, man.
>
> Tertullian

> For Adam was formed first, then Eve; and Adam was not deceived, but the woman was deceived and became a transgressor.
>
> 1 Timothy 2:13-14

'She took of its fruit and ate; and she also gave some to her husband, who was with her, and he ate.' It was not simply a bite of the fruit. The woman took and enjoyed the abundance. She took her time plucking and eating and sharing. It was not an instantaneous erroneous behaviour

---

[76] Julie Faith Parker, 'Blaming Eve Alone: Translation, Omission, and Implications of הִמָּעֵ in Genesis 3:6b' in *Journal of Biblical Literature*, Vol. 132, No. 4 (2013), pp. 733.

[77] Julie Faith Parker, 'Blaming Eve Alone: Translation, Omission, and Implications of הִמָּעֵ in Genesis 3:6b'. 747.

but one of slow indulgence. The man was also with her and he ate. They revel in the act. It is not individual sin here but communal. We collude together and we cover up together. It reminds us of the seven original sins: pride, envy, gluttony, greed, lust, wrath and sloth which have an individualistic dimension. The new modern seven sins: genetic modification, carrying out experiments on humans, polluting the environment, causing social injustice, causing poverty, becoming obscenely wealthy and taking drugs, have a social resonance and show us that our vices affect other people. The impact of our choices can be devastating.

> The oldest computer was owned by Adam and Eve.
> It was an Apple with very limited memory.
> Just 1 byte and everything crashed!

Chapter 3 names fundamental terms of the human constitution: desire, knowledge, fear, desire again, and finally difficulty. Sin and evil follow only later. Genesis 3-6 provides the outline of 'original sin' and it is named for the first time in 4:7, where it is part of a portrait of Cain. Abel as a counterbalance to Cain points to the fact that both good and evil are the human reality after Genesis 3.[78]

In Genesis, desire, not evil, seems to mark the very act of human seeing and taking the fruit. The description of the woman's action in 3:6, that 'she saw... and took', has resonances in other biblical passages suggestive of desire.

---

[78] Mark S. Smith, 'Before Human Sin and Evil: Desire and Fear in the Garden of God,' in *The Catholic Biblical Quarterly*, Vol 80, 2018:219.

- In Genesis 6:2, the divine sons 'see' how beautiful human women are and then 'take' them.
- In Genesis 12:14-15, the Egyptians 'see' how beautiful Sarah is, and so she is 'taken' into Pharaoh's palace.
- In Genesis 34:2, Shechem 'saw... and took' Dinah and then raped her.
- In 2 Samuel 11:2, 4, David 'saw' Bathsheba from the roof of his royal palace and he 'took her'.[79]

Desire precedes the knowledge of good and evil, and then fear follows in the wake of knowing good and evil. As it unfolds in Genesis 3, the story is one of human desire. We can, we want, and we will, regardless of the consequences.

To become wise is a good intention but how we go about attaining it matters. Surely the woman and man would have gained the wisdom needed from the many occasions and life forms around them, instead of by stealing.

One of the problems in the serpent beguiling the woman and man is that both had the knowledge to correctly respond to the serpent, the man more so, given the Lord God had earlier spoken directly to him about the matter. And that is the problem we all face – we have little faith in the knowledge we possess, our intuition, our know-how. We are easily swayed by what others have to say, and we see this best with social media and fake news. The key to addressing this is to trust the knowledge, experience and relationships we have and to learn the art of wisdom. The Bible is replete

---

[79] Mark S. Smith, 'Before Human Sin and Evil: Desire and Fear in the Garden of God,' 224.

with the importance of the getting of wisdom. Today the world imposes information overload, but we lack in wisdom of discernment. The getting of wisdom would send the serpent far away from us, for wisdom allows us to discern God's truth from the world's lies.

Genesis 3:7 *Then the eyes of both were opened, and they knew that they were naked; and they sewed fig leaves together and made loincloths for themselves.*

Early on in Chapter 3, the story is about seeing correctly. It questions how we see things:

- 3:5 Your eyes will be opened
- 3:6 Saw that the tree was good
- 3:6 Delight to the eyes
- 3:7 Eyes of both were opened

What do we see when we really look? If our eyes are open, do we see like God who 'saw everything… and indeed it was very good' (1:31) or are we like the woman and man who 'knew that they were naked; and they sewed fig leaves together and made loincloths for themselves' (3:7). Can we see, with eyes opened, the good in the world, or are we too self-focused to see beyond ourselves?

Prior to taking the forbidden fruit, the woman 'saw that the tree was good'. However, recognising goodness was lost after she took the fruit. It was not because she ate it, but the means of how she attained the fruit. She had taken it deceitfully, listening to the serpent.

The Lord God has created an energetic, marvellous, colourful, spectacular world. Yet the woman and man wanted more. The serpent tempts them, 'your eyes will be opened' (3:4). Yet what will they be opened to? Had they not till now enjoyed the sights of creation, their garden of Eden, their Paradise? The Lord God had taken great care, time and energy to create and was astounded by it all. We need to see with appreciation what has been given to us, otherwise we will spend our lives looking and never being satisfied, having but always desiring.

Once the serpent plants the idea in their heads that there is more to see, the woman suddenly saw the tree and its fruit 'was a delight to the eyes' (3:6). Nothing else captured or held her attention. And so it goes with all of us. How we see things and what we see depends on what our intentions are. Our hungers, lusts, ambitions, all too often distort our views. Our vision becomes too focused, too narrowed and too closed in. God has given us vistas, endless scenic views, so as not to limit our perceptions. Yet we put on blinkers and box ourselves in.

Once we get what we think is 'delightful', it becomes very different to what we expected. We see our nakedness, our shame and failures. We chose to 'be like God' (3:5) rather than build our partnership with one another and God. We chose 'knowing good and evil' (3:5) rather than seeing everything as 'very good' (1:31).

Let us compare this event with Luke's story of the Walk to Emmaus that occurs after Jesus' resurrection.

> [6]So when the woman saw that the tree was good for food, and that it was a delight to the eyes, and that the tree was to be desired to make one wise, she took of its fruit and ate; and she also gave some to

her husband, who was with her, and he ate. ⁷Then the eyes of both were opened, and they knew that they were naked; and they sewed fig leaves together and made loincloths for themselves. ⁸They heard the sound of the Lord God walking in the garden at the time of the evening breeze, and the man and his wife hid themselves from the presence of the Lord God among the trees of the garden.

Genesis 3:6-8

³⁰When he was at the table with them, he took bread, blessed and broke it, and gave it to them. ³¹Then their eyes were opened, and they recognised him; and he vanished from their sight. ³²They said to each other, 'Were not our hearts burning within us while he was talking to us on the road, while he was opening the scriptures to us?' ³³That same hour they got up and returned to Jerusalem; and they found the eleven and their companions gathered together.

Luke 24:30-32

In both cases, the eyes were opened upon eating. For the two disciples on the road to Emmaus, their eyes were able to recognise Jesus after listening to him. Their hearts burned within them. In contrast, for the woman and man, when their eyes were opened, after listening to the serpent's words, they saw they were naked. They were ashamed and hid from the Lord God.

Their sight led to shame and fear. Back in the first creation account when 'God saw', it was 'good'. The vision and perception of God is one of delight. In contrast here when 'the eyes of both were opened' (3:7), there is no recognition of goodness and beauty. How we see depends on what we hear and whom we listen to. Do our hearts burn within us as we listen to another? If it only leads to restlessness, then it is not from the Lord God.

2:17 in the day that you eat of it, you shall die
3:4 You will not die... your eyes will be open
3:7 the eyes of both were opened, and they knew that they were naked

The knowledge pursued by both woman and man seems to amount to an awareness of their nakedness. The Hebrew word for naked is 'arom' in Genesis 2:25 and the word *'arum'* is used to describe the serpent as subtle and crafty (3:1).

The placing of the tree of knowledge of good and evil in the garden can also be understood as a catalyst for humanity's development according to David James Stewart and not a test of their obedience or faithfulness. The tree was placed in the garden by the Lord God and is a 'good' aspect of creation, even if eating it brings a loss of innocence and a new knowledge of life's complexity and ambiguity.[80]

The Lord God has said they would die and they did die – but in a different way. They died to their innocence and simple way of living. The eating of the fruit enabled woman and man to cross a threshold from childlike innocence into fully differentiated ego-consciousness.

Eyes are open but what do we see? Eyes opened does not always translate to seeing correctly or 'to make one

---

[80] David James Stewart, 'The emergence of consciousness in Genesis 1–3: Jung's depth psychology and theological anthropology,' in *Zygon*, vol. 49, no. 2 (June 2014), pp. 524-525.

wise' (3:6). Wisdom and knowledge come with experience and time. The woman and man needed to experience a great deal more in life before wisdom and knowledge of good and evil would be theirs. Like us all. We will journey through life, stumbling along, encountering good and bad, experiencing positive and negative occasions.

> **Genesis 3:8** *They heard the sound of the* LORD *God walking in the garden at the time of the evening breeze, and the man and his wife hid themselves from the presence of the* LORD *God among the trees of the garden.*

To know good and evil is to accept life is a combination of beauty and suffering. The knowledge gained is not meant to be a power quest, 'you will be like God' (3:5). The knowledge gained is not meant to make us less than we are, 'They knew that they were naked; and they sewed fig leaves together' (3:7). The knowledge gained is not meant to separate, they 'hid themselves' (3:8). Rather the knowledge gained should make us more fully human.

When there is a right relationship between humans and the Lord God, the woman and man are in right relationship with each other. They are able to be themselves, to be transparent, at ease and not self-conscious in each other's presence. But when they are disconnected from the Lord God (3:17), there follows a 'dis-ease' between humans.

They heard – we do not see but we intuit the Lord God's presence. We know in our very being, in our deep core, when the Lord God is near.

Lord God walking in the garden – in our backyard, nearer than we think, seeking an informal relationship with us.

Lord God walks in the evening breeze – the time when all has slowed down and time to let go and reflect on what remains of the day. Somewhat like the Sabbath moment of each day when we are reminded once again of God's presence in our lives and in all creation. Who walks in the evening breeze if not lovers, hand in hand, amorously together, whispering secret nothings? The Lord God makes a lover's appearance at this very time. Lord God, our lover, our hearts delight, and joy. If you do not step out into the evening breeze you will miss the sight and sounds and your soul's awakening. Take notice of the Lord God who loves your very presence. To rest after a long day, to lean on the Lord God. Late into the night... lost in love.

The Lord God comes as our friend, to be with us, to walk in the garden and spend time with the woman and man. No matter how hard we try to 'hide' and 'cover up', ultimately, we have to 'face' the Lord God and ourselves.

Why is it we cannot talk to the Lord God face to face, heart to heart? What holds us back from being open and honest? The Lord God is perhaps too good and too loving and too perfect for us. An encounter that may be too painful and too truthful for our convenience.

The Lord God comes walking in the cool of the day but where was the Lord God when we were tempted by the serpent? Where is God in our troubles? We are quick to blame the Lord God for not helping us but then again why were not our thoughts turned to Lord God when it mattered? The Lord God is often an after-thought, or an inconvenience.

But the Lord God walks gently on the earth, quietly in the evening breeze. So should we. God invites us to walk in the garden. The gift of life is here. Walk slowly and softly, tread gently on this earth, be pleasantly surprised.

The Lord God searches for us but are we searching for God, or have we abandoned God? Searching but no response or a reluctant one at best. We are eager to hide away. God searching. Who needs whom? Who hides their face from whom?

In the woman and man's rejection of prohibitions, their casting away of restrictions, their throwing off of limitations, the Lord God still remains and is yet not done away with. When boundaries have been overstepped, the Lord God still remains beyond the boundaries. When all is said and done, the Lord God continues to be present. When all is given up and irrevocably changed, God still remains and walks out to meet us. And perhaps, just perhaps, those who butt heads with the Lord God of the now, are the very ones who will walk with the Lord God of tomorrow.

The Lord God continues, even when we think we have outdone and out-grown God. Even when we have cast off God, gone out on a limb, chosen otherwise, blatantly misbehaved, diverged deliberately, God is never left behind. The Lord God is on the move, and no matter our paths, our choices, our beliefs, our ways, our thinking, in the end we always come face to face with the Lord God, who is bigger than our revolutionary ways, rebellious thoughts, obstinate decisions. Even when we think we are being radical in our behaviour, ultimately it is only a small step forward and the Lord God comes along and picks us up in God's stride, to set us down again further on in our journey.

Before the praise and glory and honour, before the bells, whistles and incense, there was just humans and God, alone in the garden, befriended. Our yearning is to restore that relationship, that time of companionship. In speaking honestly and openly, deeply and lovingly, with one another, we can once again relive paradise.

Genesis 3:9 *But the* LORD *God called to the man, and said to him, 'Where are you?'*

The Lord God calls to the man, not to the woman, because the man had heard the prohibition and was responsible. God asks, 'Where are you?' It is not a question the Creator of all would need an answer to. God knows where we are. Yet the question is directed to the man, and to each of us, 'Where are you?'

God is asking for us because we seem to be absent. Where are you? Do we recognise we are in the garden of Eden? God is asking us, do we know the gifts given to us? The places we can call our very own, our home? Are we where we are meant to be or have we become a foreigner to ourselves and our surroundings? Where are we because the Lord God wants us home and back in embrace. 'The LORD God called' (3:9) and will always call (Mark 1:16-20; John 1:43).

I have called you by name, you are mine.

Isaiah 43:1

God calls, and calls, and calls... waiting for a response. And how many times have we called to God? There are endless situations of God calling out to us and we in turn calling out to God.

We call to God in our need.

> Give ear to my prayer, O God; do not hide yourself from my supplication.
>
> Psalm 55:1
> (also see Job 10:1-2 and Psalm 17:1)

We call out to God in praise and thanksgiving.

> I call upon the Lord, who is worthy to be praised; so I shall be saved from my enemies.
>
> Psalm 18:3
> (also see Psalms 103:1 and 138:1)

And God always responds in graciousness.

> O Lord, you have searched me and known me. You know when I sit down and when I rise up; you discern my thoughts from far away.
>
> Psalm 139:1-2

To be called is to feel that there is someone out there who knows us and is asking about us. We are not alone. The Lord God did not create a world teeming with life for us to turn our backs on and to dwell in solitary misery. Lord God calls us to abandon our own self-centredness and once again return and embrace life and relationships. When we shun the world because of our narrowed vision, we harm our better and greater selves. Life is a world of opportunities. Do not reduce the possibilities.

The Lord God offers what no one else can – an assurance of life and love – and calls us by name, not to condemn, but to seek our company. Yet so much drowns out the call:

- Our shame
- Our self-hatred
- Our busyness
- Our temptations
- Our Streaming addiction
- Our gaming addiction
- Our fitness regime
- Our workload
- Our problems
- Our social media pages

Yet the Lord God is walking in the garden with us, calling us in our everyday life. The woman and man had drifted away and so it is with all of us. There will be times when we stray, venture out and leave paradise. We will find stepping out on our own is a great teacher, and that life ahead can be a challenge. But that is all part of growing up. The important point to remember is that the Lord God never loses us on the way. We can always return home because the Lord God is calling out to us, 'Where are you?' For our part, are we prepared to respond?

> **Genesis 3:10-11** *He said, 'I heard the sound of you in the garden, and I was afraid, because I was naked; and I hid myself.'* [11] *He said, 'Who told you that you were naked? Have you eaten from the tree of which I commanded you not to eat?'*

Neither did the man admit to his nakedness, nor did he admit to breaking the commandment. He would not admit his shame or error. Today, people do not sin, they just choose differently and change courses. We are free to choose what we want to do and who is to judge us. And when we err, we can get ourselves back on track. It is really no big deal. Maybe so, but do we give any thought to the consequences along the way, the impact our decisions have on ourselves and others? The relationships that we damage and the trust we lose? Too quick to brush away our errors and get on with life, we have forgotten to stop, reflect and be honest about who we are, what we have done, where we are heading and how.

> He felt only an immense disappointment because he had to go to God empty-handed, with nothing done at all. It seemed to him, at that moment, that it would have been quite easy to have been a saint. It would only have needed a little self-restraint and a little courage. He felt like someone who has missed happiness by seconds at an appointed place. He knew now that at the end there was only one thing that counted – to be a saint.
>
> Graham Greene[81]

We need to stop and decide – do we need God in our lives or not? It reminds us of the great parable of the prodigal son, where the younger son takes off only to find that it is best to return home to the father.

---

[81] Graham Greene, *The Power and the Glory*, new edn, (London: William Heinemann and Bodley Head, 1971), 251.

> [17] But when he came to himself he said, "How many of my father's hired hands have bread enough and to spare, but here I am dying of hunger! [18] I will get up and go to my father, and I will say to him, 'Father, I have sinned against heaven and before you; [19] I am no longer worthy to be called your son; treat me like one of your hired hands.'"
>
> Luke 15:17-19

What is our reaction when we hear the Lord God? In the Creation account, woman and man hide, using the excuse they were naked. We hide behind a false sense of morality in order not to face the real truth. And we all do it. We cover our shame with lies. We cast the blame elsewhere to avoid the truth.

The man did not hide because he was ashamed of his nakedness, given the fact he had spent his life naked in the garden and conversing with the Lord God. The man hid in order to avoid admitting the truth about what he had done. The man says to the Lord God that he was afraid.

If the man had been honest with God, he would not have had to face the messy consequences. The web of lies we weave, trap us in misery.

The movement into adulthood changes the way we view life and how we choose to live. The woman and man have reached adulthood. Their view of the world has become more sceptical and wary. There is a loss of innocence in becoming an adult. We lose our simplicity and spontaneity.

The Lord God sees through the lies to expose the truth. The man accounts for his hiding from the Lord God, using the excuse of his nakedness, but Lord God is not fooled.

Immediately the Lord God gets to the crux of the matter. First, asking who has been playing with the man's mind. Secondly, questioning if the man did what he was explicitly told not to. And that is who the Lord God is – the one who leads us to the truth.

Yet the man does not respond to the question, 'Who told you that you were naked?' It is not a question we can blame on another. What shame we have is ours alone. And it is we who must examine our personal image, our perception of ourselves. Negative image does us harm. We forget we were made in God's image. And the Lord God reminds the man of such, 'Who told you that you were naked?' The Lord God does not agree with the man that he is naked and needs to cover himself. There is no shame before God. Yet we lie to hide our shame. We play the blame game.

> **Genesis 3:12** *The man said, 'The woman whom you gave to be with me, she gave me fruit from the tree, and I ate'.*

From the woman being a helper and partner, and from being 'bone of my bones and flesh of my flesh' (2:18, 23), the man now describes her as 'the woman whom you gave to be with me' (3:12). A loss of respect and intimacy has occurred. The man hides behind his error by casting the blame on the very one he was meant to 'cling' to and 'become one flesh' with (2:24). There is now a sudden change of heart and a degree of alienation between the man and the Lord God, and the man and the woman. How fickle we are! One minute we proclaim our deep love and care for another but, when the going gets tough, we cast the other off without hesitation. We cannot and do not admit we have made an error.

Yes, the woman gave the man the fruit from the tree, but the man had been told by God from the beginning, 'You may freely eat of every tree of the garden; but of the tree of the knowledge of good and evil you shall not eat, for in the day that you eat of it you shall die' (2:16-17). And the man had told the woman for she responds to the serpent, that God said, 'you shall not eat of the fruit of the tree that is in the middle of the garden, nor shall you touch it, or you shall die' (3:3). They both knew the consequences.

Perhaps the man thought if the woman gave him the fruit, he would be less guilty, because he was not the one to take the fruit off the tree. Yet he still played the game, no matter the level of participation. Once you are in, you are in.

> Let your word be 'Yes, Yes' or 'No, No'; anything more than this comes from the evil one.
>
> Matthew 5:37

Yet the man responds to the question with some grain of truth. He was with the woman, whom the Lord God 'gave to be with me'. The man was doing the right thing by being with the woman created for him as a partner and the man continues, 'she gave me fruit from the tree, and I ate'. The woman did give him fruit and he did what was expected, eat the fruit. So, the man has justified himself.

The only problem is that the man did everything the woman asked but the man had forgotten all that the Lord God asked. So, what is truth? How do we discern what is right and what is wrong? Just as the serpent misrepresented the Lord God's words, so does the man. We are spin doctors, so good at distorting meaning to cover up our failures and inconsistencies. And we convince ourselves constantly of our self-righteousness. But ultimately the voice we should listen to is the voice of the Lord God, that all too often is forgotten or drowned out by voices that appeal more to us.

There is an educational tool that asks 5 *Whys* in assisting students to reach the correct answers to questions. They keep asking why until they get to the very crux of the issue at hand. Perhaps rather than just applying it to external problems that require a solution, we should question our own actions. So, the Lord God asks the man 'Why'. This is what follows:

1. Why – Because the woman was with me
2. Why – The woman gave me the fruit
3. Why – I was told to eat it
4. Why – I was hungry
5. Why – Maybe I wanted to be like God?

The man's greatest fault was to behave in a way that shrugged off responsibility in favour of something more sensual. So what have we to say then of the woman?

Genesis 3:13 *Then the* LORD *God said to the woman, 'What is this that you have done?' The woman said, 'The serpent tricked me, and I ate'.*

God then turns to the woman and asks, 'What is this that you have done?' (3:13). A piercing question that goes right to the heart. What is it that we choose to do and then suffer the consequences for? Unless we are confronted with the reality of our decision-making, we will continue to deny any fault in our choices and actions. What we do will be seen and questioned. There is accountability. By examining our choices and why we make them, we learn and grow. If we do not stop and question ourselves, we continue on heedlessly.

The woman speaks for herself but does not try to implicate the man. She admits, 'The serpent tricked me, and I ate' (3:13). The woman rightly says it is the serpent who is the tempter, not she herself. But the woman, like the man, speaks only part of the truth. She uses the excuse 'the serpent tricked me and I ate', but she fails to mention the rest of her reasons. The blame is shifted from one to another. And it continues on and on. So again, let us apply the 5 whys. The woman responds:

1. Why – The serpent tempted me
2. Why – I saw the tree was good for fruit
3. Why – I saw it was a delight to the eyes
4. Why – It would make me wise
5. Why – I wanted to eat and share it with the man

Her intentions and reasoning are not wrong. She had hoped to enjoy the beauty of the fruit and to gain wisdom. It was not a power grab on her behalf. It was a desire to enjoy further possibilities. Yet the Lord God stops us and asks us to take a really good look at ourselves, not to pass judgment but to nudge us in the right direction.

The Lord God will come in the midst of our disasters and sort things out – but of course sorting out the mess we created will require pain. As they say, no pain, no gain. The Lord God will lead us to better choices by walking with us, by our side, even if we are shamed of our very own selves.

Assured of the Lord God's constant watchful eye, let us amuse ourselves with the following 'take' on the story.

A modern take of the story: God, Adam and Eve

After creating heaven and earth, God created Adam and Eve. And the first thing he said was 'DON'T!'

'Don't what?' Adam replied.

'Don't eat the forbidden fruit,' God said.

'Forbidden fruit? We have forbidden fruit? Hey Eve... we have forbidden fruit!'

'No way!'

'Yes way!'

'Do NOT eat the fruit!' said God.

'Why?'

'Because I am your Father and I said so!' God replied, wondering why He hadn't stopped creation after making the elephants. A few minutes later, God saw His children having an apple break and he was angry! 'Didn't I tell you not to eat the fruit?' God asked.

'Uh huh,' Adam replied.

'Then why did you?' said the Father.

'I don't know,' said Eve.

'She started it!' Adam said

'Did not!'

'Did too!'

'DID NOT!'

Having had it with the two of them, God's punishment was that Adam and Eve should have children of their own. Thus the pattern was set and it has never changed. But there is reassurance in the story! If you have persistently and lovingly tried to give children wisdom and they haven't taken it, don't be hard on yourself. If God had trouble raising children, what makes you think it would be a piece of cake for you?

Chapter 8

We can begin again

Genesis 3:14-24

^{14}*The* L*ord* *God said to the serpent,*

> *'Because you have done this,*
>   *cursed are you among all animals*
>   *and among all wild creatures;*
> *upon your belly you shall go,*
>   *and dust you shall eat*
>   *all the days of your life.*
> ^{15}*I will put enmity between you and the woman,*
>   *and between your offspring and hers;*
> *he will strike your head,*
>   *and you will strike his heel.'*

^{16}*To the woman he said,*

> *'I will greatly increase your pangs in childbearing;*
>   *in pain you shall bring forth children,*
> *yet your desire shall be for your husband,*
>   *and he shall rule over you.'*

^{17}*And to the man he said,*

> 'Because you have listened to the voice of your wife,
>   and have eaten of the tree
> about which I commanded you,
>   "You shall not eat of it",
> cursed is the ground because of you;
>   in toil you shall eat of it all the days of your life;
> [18] thorns and thistles it shall bring forth for you;
>   and you shall eat the plants of the field.
> [19] By the sweat of your face
>   you shall eat bread
> until you return to the ground,
>   for out of it you were taken;
> you are dust,
>   and to dust you shall return.'

[20] *The man named his wife Eve, because she was the mother of all who live.* [21] *And the* LORD *God made garments of skins for the man and for his wife, and clothed them.*

[22] *Then the* LORD *God said, 'See, the man has become like one of us, knowing good and evil; and now, he might reach out his hand and take also from the tree of life, and eat, and live for ever'—* [23] *therefore the* LORD *God sent him forth from the garden of Eden, to till the ground from which he was taken.* [24] *He drove out the man; and at the east of the garden of Eden he placed the cherubim, and a sword flaming and turning to guard the way to the tree of life.*

When the serpent, woman and man collude against the Lord God's command, the Lord God does not baulk or hide away or avoid confrontation. The first thing the Lord God does is ask questions to ascertain the truth. Only when the

Lord God hears the man and the woman out is appropriate action taken. Truth cannot be silenced, and the Lord God takes a stand. Deceit needs to be exposed, lies need to cease and repercussions must lead to a change of heart.

Genesis 3:14-15 *The* LORD *God said to the serpent, 'Because you have done this, cursed are you among all animals and among all wild creatures; upon your belly you shall go, and dust you shall eat all the days of your life.* ^{15}*I will put enmity between you and the woman, and between your offspring and hers; he will strike your head, and you will strike his heel.'*

The Lord God does not shy away from the serpent but stamps out the one who sought to cause mischief and harm. It is a message for us also, to silence and disable those who choose to wreak havoc and destruction, who hide behind lies and encourage deceitful actions that undermine the good. Evil should not be allowed to have its way in the world.

The serpent is a sign of temptation, deceitfulness, lies and trouble-making. And the punishment is to be 'cursed' – to move about 'upon your belly' – and to eat 'dust'. Not a pretty picture but it does capture the futileness of pursuing evil. Living a lie becomes a life drained of goodness, empty of hope and enveloped in bitterness and darkness. It destroys our very selves. We lose trust, suspicion crawls in, jealousy and anger clutch at us, and we become devoid of inner peace. Life becomes a constant game of covering up, manipulating and deceiving.

The state of such a one who deliberately pursues evil intentions condemns themselves to a cursed life, refusing to recognise the blessings around them. Surrounded by a garden paradise, the evil focuses on the prohibition and not the opportunities. A life moving upon their belly, refusing to look up and around, to acknowledge light and beauty. They choose darkness, to slither through life, hiding, sneaking, avoiding and unable to face reality.

Finally, 'dust you shall eat'. A bitter, dry life, where enjoyment and desire have escaped. One wallows in anger, hatred, with a distaste for beauty and life.

When Jesus said to Satan, 'Get behind me,' he was acknowledging that we all live with the devil. We cannot escape evil but as long as we are in front and evil is behind us, in our shadow, we are protected.

Looking at this verse from another context, it was understood that the serpent would bruise the heel of Adam and Eve's descendent, who would in turn bruise its head, referring to King David, who crushed the Moabites, who worshipped their god in the form of a snake.

> He also defeated the Moabites and, making them lie down on the ground, measured them off with a cord; he measured two lengths of cord for those who were to be put to death, and one length for those who were to be spared. And the Moabites became servants to David and brought tribute.
>
> 2 Samuel 8:2

This reminds us of the earlier creation myths where the gods destroyed their enemies who often took the form of a serpent.

So the Lord God now assesses the position of the humans, not simply from the fact that they ate the forbidden fruit but:

- Were easily tempted
- Chose to heed the voice of a serpent in preference to the Lord God
- That both the woman and man did not positively support each other
- Struggled to discern right from wrong
- Lied
- Thought they could hide
- Covered up their wrong doings
- Deceived themselves, arguing nakedness was the problem
- Distorted the truth
- Believed they should know as much as the Lord God

The Lord God had created female and male in God's image. Woman and man were created to help one another. God does not impose discord between them. They have allowed themselves to fall into such a state and they must be responsible enough to work towards creating a partnership that once again gives importance to one another and to the Lord God. The Lord God is indeed one of constant patience in the face of human mess!

> **Genesis 3:16** *To the woman he said, 'I will greatly increase your pangs in childbearing; in pain you shall bring forth children, yet your desire shall be for your husband, and he shall rule over you'.*

Common to both the woman and man is 'difficulty'. The woman will suffer pain or difficulty in childbirth (3:16), and the man will suffer the difficulty of the now cursed ground (3:17). The consequences for the woman stand in between those detailed for the serpent and the man.

- Childbirth becomes agonising for her
- What was once mutual desire and delight between her and the man is now gone
- Worse yet, her man now rules over her

It is a sad predicament we bring upon ourselves when partners are unfaithful towards one another, when they tread life burdened with guilt and shamed by sin, that finds its outward expression in abusive ways.

The verse continues on, 'your desire shall be for your husband, and he shall rule over you'. When a man rules over a woman, this opposes the original intention of partnership. To desire one is to open ourselves to another. When we know another desires us, we feel a sense of power over them but also the invitation to open ourselves vulnerably.

In a close reading of the text within the context of peasant life in the Iron Age, Carol Meyers understands 3:16 as explaining the hardships for women who had to bear many children so that there would be several viable offspring for cultivating the fields, caring for aging parents, and to inherit the land. The man's mastery over woman is only with regard to sexual relations so that the agrarian household would have sufficient offspring.[82]

---

[82] Carol Meyers, *Rediscovering Eve: Ancient Israelite Women in Context*, (New York: Oxford University Press, 2013), 81-102.

In biblical times and for centuries on, infant mortality was very high. Women gave birth to many children and in the process underwent much pain. Not mentioned here, aside from the physical pain, was the emotional suffering of mothers and fathers, when their children died at birth or at a young age. And yet, giving birth to new life is a hoped for experience. Woman and man continue to beget life as the desire for family is strong.

> If you heed these ordinances, by diligently observing them, the LORD your God will maintain with you the covenant loyalty that he swore to your ancestors; [13]he will love you, bless you, and multiply you; he will bless the fruit of your womb and the fruit of your ground, your grain and your wine and your oil, the increase of your cattle and the issue of your flock, in the land that he swore to your ancestors to give you. [14]You shall be the most blessed of peoples, with neither sterility nor barrenness among you or your livestock.
>
> Deuteronomy 7:12-14

Consider humans and the many struggles they go through to have children. It is a difficult time for couples when they cannot fall pregnant and they try various methods to assist. The giving of birth is also painful and yet the gift of miraculous new life erases all else. God said to multiply, but not just to propagate numbers for the survival of a species. To multiply is to bring joy and meaning to one's own life. To nurture life, flesh from one's flesh, is to discover the power to love another deeply, totally and unselfishly.

Yes, entry into this world is painful but also a blessing. A reminder that life is not smooth sailing. There is pain, toil and trouble, but there is also joy, wonder and blessings.

The woman and man wished to 'know good and evil'. Knowledge in its truest sense is not factual knowledge 'about' something; it is direct experience of it. The woman and man could not know good and evil without experiencing these things directly, so they were cast out of the garden of bliss and sent into a world where food comes through hard work and where childbirth is painful and dangerous. Both the woman and man will experience difficulties in life.

> **Genesis 3:17-18** *And to the man he said, 'Because you have listened to the voice of your wife, and have eaten of the tree about which I commanded you, "You shall not eat of it", cursed is the ground because of you; in toil you shall eat of it all the days of your life; 18 thorns and thistles it shall bring forth for you; and you shall eat the plants of the field.*

For the first time, the woman is referred to as 'wife.' Yet she is not so named by her husband but by the Lord God. The man only referred to her as 'the woman' in 3:13, to de-identify himself from her. Yet, that is not so easily achieved. The woman and man are wife and husband, and remain so, in good times and in those times where their choices have put them to shame. Failures and mistakes do not qualify as excuses to renege on one's relationship. She remains his wife, even though they deceived each other. He will remain her husband even though they veered onto the wrong path. The relationship must bear the ups and downs, otherwise it is not a relationship but a marriage of convenience. And the man soon realises that is the truth.

The man had two opportunities to consider what was being said and to cease from wrong decision-making. The man could have rebuked the serpent for misinterpreting what the Lord God said, but he did not. He could have responded to the woman who offered him the fruit and advised otherwise. Again, he did not.

The man listened to the voice of the woman. It is an attack on listening to 'the voice', a listening that lacks discernment. It is simply nodding one's agreement because there is a voice in one's ear, without considering what the voice is saying, without contributing to the thought process.

When we fail to truly listen and think things through, indeed life will be a curse, life will be 'in toil' and what we experience is like 'thorns and thistles'. The man ignored the advice from the Lord God, to his own detriment.

The Lord God states to the man, 'Because you have... eaten of the tree' then 'cursed is the ground because of you'. The Lord God does not curse the ground. It is the man that has cursed himself. He chose to go his own way, and as such life becomes dry, difficult and barren. The ground yields a curse because of humans' inappropriate control of the ground.

We have taken too much from the ground, stolen the earth's resources, hungered for more, eaten the earth's fruits as gluttons, ravished the earth, and now we face the serious consequences of our greed. Arable land is diminishing, fertile soil is depleting, luscious evergreens are destroyed and the ground is cursed because of us.

Humans hungered for knowledge of evil and this craving led to a lifestyle of work, money, greed, consumerism, materialism, ambition, recognition, success, value, profit margins; so we worked and worked to get more of what we did not need, forgetting that what we had been given already was more than enough. And humans continue to work and struggle to satisfy their insatiable hunger and die before they ever realise they had a garden of Eden to enjoy.

One now only lives to work, as the passage puts it, 'in toil you shall eat of it all the days of your life'. When we turn our face from Lord God, we leave ourselves without the promise of hope, the gift of blessings. Life becomes a survival of the fittest, a competition to attain all I can, no matter how. Yet, David Attenborough's recent documentary *The Year the Earth Changed* remarkably visualises how earth with all its inhabitants can live wonderfully if only humans were not destructive in their lifestyle choices.

The Lord God is not punishing but stating the obvious. Women suffer in child bearing and in relationship to men. Men face work that can be difficult and unrewarding. Humans have a life that can be blessed but also requires greater effort on their part if they are to live fully.

> When in disgrace with fortune and men's eyes
> I all alone beweep my outcast state,
> And trouble deaf heaven with my bootless cries,
> And look upon myself, and curse my fate,
> Wishing me like to one more rich in hope,
> Featured like him, like him with friends possessed,
> Desiring this man's art, and that man's scope,
> With what I most enjoy contented least;
> Yet in these thoughts my self almost despising,

Haply I think on thee, and then my state,
Like to the lark at break of day arising
From sullen earth, sings hymns at heaven's gate;
For thy sweet love remembered such wealth brings
That then I scorn to change my state with kings.

Shakespeare – Sonnet xxix 4-8

Despite 'consuming' knowledge, it does not obliterate reality for the woman and man, who experience difficulties of childbearing and work that is tiring and unrewarding. Knowledge does not do away with the mundane, everyday task of living. Knowledge does not remove suffering.

Genesis 3:19 *By the sweat of your face you shall eat bread until you return to the ground, for out of it you were taken; you are dust, and to dust you shall return.*

In chapter 3, the Lord God tells the man that he will work in the fields but never receive a proper recompense for the difficult work he does. The man is cursed in relationship to the ground. 'Earth' (*'adamah*) is not the general Hebrew word for 'Earth' (*'erets*) but the word for 'arable land'. Work itself is not a punishment as man had worked in the garden of Eden. The punishment upon man was that now the work would be frustrating.

[13]You were in Eden, the garden of God;
  every precious stone was your covering,
carnelian, chrysolite, and moonstone,
    beryl, onyx, and jasper,
sapphire, turquoise, and emerald;
  and worked in gold were your settings
  and your engravings.

> On the day that you were created
>   they were prepared.
> ¹⁴With an anointed cherub as guardian I placed you;
>   you were on the holy mountain of God;
>   you walked among the stones of fire.
> ¹⁵You were blameless in your ways
>   from the day that you were created,
>   until iniquity was found in you.
> ¹⁶In the abundance of your trade
>   you were filled with violence, and you sinned;
> so I cast you as a profane thing from the mountain of God,
>   and the guardian cherub drove you out
>   from among the stones of fire.
> ¹⁷Your heart was proud because of your beauty;
>   you corrupted your wisdom for the sake of your splendour.
> I cast you to the ground;
>   I exposed you before kings,
>   to feast their eyes on you.
> ¹⁸By the multitude of your iniquities,
>   in the unrighteousness of your trade,
>   you profaned your sanctuaries.
> So I brought out fire from within you;
>   it consumed you,
> and I turned you to ashes on the earth
>   in the sight of all who saw you.
>
> Ezekiel 28:13-18

And as a reminder once again to humans with a tendency to forget, the Lord God proclaims, 'You are dust and to dust you shall return' (Genesis 3:19; Ecclesiastes 3:20). Humans are from the *humus*. Yes, life is given and life is taken from us, but in-between is a lifetime of growing up that we are called to do. It is the in-between time that matters. It is a journey towards creating.

> The harmony between the Creator, humanity and creation as a whole was disrupted by our presuming to take the place of God and refusing to acknowledge our creaturely limitations. This in turn distorted our mandate to 'have dominion' over the earth (Genesis 1:28), to 'till it and keep it' (Genesis 2:15). As a result, the originally harmonious relationship between human beings and nature became conflictual (Genesis 3:17-19).
>
> Pope Francis[83]

The Lord God does not put the blame on the man, nor the woman, nor the serpent. The blame is placed on all three. It does not matter what excuses and how many excuses we come up with, ultimately we each have to take responsibility for our choices. As painful as it might appear, we have to take an honest look at ourselves and see where we went wrong, how we went wrong, and what steps now need to be taken to return to where we ought to be. Perhaps the uplifting side of all this is that there is a way to solve our current mess, and we can always begin again, by acknowledging that the Lord God's ever caring presence remains constantly beside us.

---

[83] Pope Francis Encyclical on Climate Change 2015 *Laudato Si'* (*Praise be to you my Lord*), paragraph 66. http://m.vatican.va/content/francescomobile/en/encyclicals/documents/papa-francesco_20150524_enciclica-laudato-si.html

The reality we actually live is a paradise lost. A world now, where the Lord God is excluded, where lies abound, where the serpent's words have more clout than the wisdom of God. It is a deceiving world where it often feels the good are ridiculed, truth is distorted, the blame game is incessant, injustice rules, where taking matters more than giving, where self justification is at any cost, honest hard labour is taxed, deception wins, violence is unleashed, revenge is applauded, human life matters less, wealth yields power, playing victim is encouraged, effort is avoided, commitment is shrugged off. Troubled, chaotic, immoral, godless and self centred. A graceless world.

Thorns and thistles, sweat, dust, a landscape of the heart devoid of love. A humanity without a moral compass. Heading nowhere but self deceiving in that we are going places. And God waits. Paradise waits. Humanity... what do we want? Cast out of Paradise, into a world of pain and suffering, harshness, dry, cold, loveless, foreign, challenging, difficult, deceitful, godless... can we awaken memory of paradise? It is now our time to recreate, co-create Paradise. Woman and man must once again put aside differences and work side by side in the journey called life. Forgiveness can happen, relationships can work out.

Genesis 3:20 *The man named his wife Eve, because she was the mother of all who live.*

The Hebrew word *hawwah* or *hawwˆa*, from which 'Eve' derives, means 'life'. Thus, the man names his wife Eve, because she was 'mother of all who live'. The name is closely related to the word for snake, *hiwyˆa*.

The name Eve is a title, indicating woman is called to be alive in the world, responsible and essential. The naming of woman as Eve is an honouring of her role in creating future generations. To be mother of all is to take care and responsibility for life. To nurture and comfort, love and watch over. Originally the man was meant to be responsible for all things when God 'formed every animal of the field and every bird of the air, and brought them to the man to see what he would call them' (2:19). Now the man shares this responsibility with the woman.

The man recognises that woman must complement him and only together can they fulfil their responsibility in the world. There comes a point in time when we realise life is fraught with many challenges and what we thought we could do on our own becomes impossible. We realise we are not so perfect, we have our faults and shortcomings and that in order to achieve what is required of us, is to acknowledge our need for support from others.

More so, the world calls us to fullness of life, to be as mother 'parent' in the unfolding of creation. To be fully life-giving, protect, coax, love and renew. This is despite our past, our errors and our temptations.

Yet, there are two different accounts of the way the first man gives name to the first woman.

> [23]Then the man said,
> 'This at last is bone of my bones
> and flesh of my flesh
> this one shall be called Woman,
> for out of Man this one was taken.'
>
> Genesis 2:23

> The man named his wife Eve, because she was the mother of all who live.
>
> Genesis 3:20

In the first, the man emphasises their similarities – she is 'bone of my bones, and flesh of my flesh'. She was in the man's eyes, an extension of himself. In the second, he emphasises the difference. She can give birth, he cannot. When the man gives the woman a proper name, he recognises for the first time that she is different from him and that she can do something he will never do.[84] She, not he, would give birth. In this respect, she was more like God than he could be.

There is a spiritual dimension to the physical relationship between husband and wife. At one level, it is the most animal of desires, but at another it is as close as we come to the principle of divine creativity itself, namely, that love creates life, as Rabbi Jonathan Sacks affirms. That is when the man turned to his wife and for the first time saw her as a person. He himself had not had a proper name until this point either. It is only after he confers a proper name on the woman that the man acquires one himself and realises he can defeat mortality by engraving his ideals on the hearts of his children, and they on theirs, unto the end of time.[85]

---

[84] Rabbi Sacks, *Covenant & Conversation. The Genesis of Love* (Bereishit 5780), 23 October, 2019 https://rabbisacks.org/wp-content/uploads/2019/10/CC-5780-The-Genesis-of-Love-Bereishit-5780-2.pdf

[85] Rabbi Jonathan Sacks, *Covenant and Conversation: A weekly reading of the Jewish Bible. Genesis: The Book of Beginnings*, (New Milford, USA: Maggid Books, 2009), 35-36.

Genesis 3:21 *And the* Lord *God made garments of skins for the man and for his wife, and clothed them.*

We cannot hide from ourselves, nor from others and least of all from the Lord God. And the Lord God does not want to cast us off in our misery but seeks to offer us guidance. So the Lord God finds a way to forgive and make special provisions for the woman and man by giving of animal clothes.

In 3:7 we read:

> and they sewed fig leaves together and made loincloths for themselves.

And in 3:21 we read:

> And the Lord God made garments of skins for the man and for his wife, and clothed them.

It is the Lord God that provides the know-how, the help, the 'covering' and 'protection' humans need on their journey. Recall in the first Creation account, 'God blessed them' (1:28). Ever in subtle ways, humans are 'watched over' by God.

As in the modern world, clothes in Genesis 3 may have had multiple associations:

- Traditionally been associated with sexuality
- In the context of ancient Near Eastern creation stories, clothes were a symbolic recognition of human difference from other animals, who do not need clothes

- Likeness to gods, who wore clothes in ancient Near Eastern iconography
- By specifying that the clothes are 'skins,' Genesis offers a recognition of human dependence on other animals

Today, the fashion industry profits on human vulnerabilities by convincing us that the latest fashion and labels can make us erase our insecurities. God also makes clothes, 'garments of skins' (3:21), but it is practical wear that offers warmth and protection from the natural elements. So how we use clothes to express who we are is very powerful. It can cover our shame, add confidence, prepare us for the day's work and protect us from the weather.

Beneath our ravenous appetites and our extravagant attire, who are we really? The real question is, can we stand naked before God without shame?

In 3:7, the sewing of fig leaves is an early stage of maturation into adulthood, of caring for oneself and others. In 3:21, the Lord God makes garments of skin, which is a more durable material. The use of animals for clothing emerges here and we see a progression in human practice. The woman and man are now dressed in 'fine' clothes. This occurs immediately after the Lord God describes the suffering they will endure for the choices they made. There is now no turning back. By making garments for them, the Lord God is assisting the woman and man on their journey as adults in a difficult world. Without the subtle assistance, humans would struggle. Yet God will accommodate their needs.

It sounds as if it comes from a world where sorrow is perfectly ordinary, but still there is more to be said... Everything you fear is true. And yet. Everything you have done wrong, you have done really wrong. And yet. And yet... Shut up and listen, and let yourself count, just a little bit, on a calm that you do not have to make for yourself, because here it is, freely offered.

Francis Spufford[86]

The Lord God forgives over and over again, despite the harm done, the pain suffered, the innocence lost, the humiliation faced, the trust withdrawn, the goodness overshadowed, and the hope shattered.

Uncleanness arrived not from material contagion but from the disturbed desire that people conceive to pollute and do harm to themselves. Uncleanness had to be dealt with in the inward, spiritual personality of those afflicted. The Lord God's Spirit was a far more vital force than the serpent's that disturbed humanity. Against demonic infection a greater, counter contagion could prevail, the positive energy of God's purity.[87]

When the storm passes
I ask you Lord, in shame
that you return us better,
as you once dreamed us.

Alexis Valdes, 'Hope'

---

[86] Francis Spufford, *Unapologetic: Why, Despite Everything, Christianity can still make a surprising emotional sense*, (London: Faber, 2012), 16.
[87] Bruce Chilton, 'Kingdom of God' in *The New Testament and Ethics. A Book-by-Book survey*, Joel B. Green, Editor, Grand Rapids, Michigan: Baker Academics, 2013, (100-108).

Immediately after providing the clothes, the Lord God says, 'the man has become like one of us, knowing good and evil' (3:22). The Hebrew words translated 'good and bad' are often translated 'good and evil', but the Hebrew indicates knowledge broader than just moral discernment.

So there is the threat that humans become like God, knowing good and evil, and possibly achieving eternal life! That is surely a threat as we have seen throughout human history, with the reckless pursuit of knowledge, power, and the fountain of youth. The problem here is that humans are not gods, and their knowing good and evil is not handled as the Lord God would. Our choices can incline towards evil and such consequences can be devastating for not only humans but the entire earth. This would be a greater catastrophe if humans were to attain eternal life. Yet, unlike other ancient creation stories which tell of how the gods tried to keep human beings from attaining immortality, the Genesis account has the Lord God provide access to the tree of life.

Evil will only be overcome by God. Human nature remains all too fickle. An unbounded hunger to reach out for more, for power, knowledge and eternal life.

What is it to have more knowledge, greater power and eternal life? The Lord God has it all but uses it for a greater good. The Lord God displays creativity, beauty, compassion and love. What we do with our ever-growing consciousness, our hungry minds and thirsting souls, must matter.

In knowing good and evil there is always risk and temptation. Do we lean towards the good or as God hints, 'he might reach out his hand and take also from the tree of life' (3:22)? Does our life become the only life that matters?

Morality and ethical decisions are part and parcel of our ever developing lives. Life is no longer black or white. Discernment and decision-making play a significant role in where we are heading. If we want to 'eat, and live forever', we do not want to create of ourselves a dracula who only lives at the cost of the life blood of others.

And why this desire to live on and on with a voraciousness that is never appeased and a need to grasp and have control of a limited destiny, when eternal life is another possibility that we should reach out for.

'Reach out his hand and take.' It is not necessarily an incorrect move. To reach out is to go beyond limited confines and to stretch further. Curiosity sends us forth. But to reach out can be for reasons of taking or giving. There is the story of one very miserly man who fell into a well and could not get out. Along comes another who leans over and calls, 'Stretch out your hand so I can pull you up.' The man in the well, miser that he was, refused to stretch out his hand, replying, 'Give me your hand instead.' So one reached out his hand to save, the other reached out to take.

In Michelangelo's painting, both God and man reach out their hands to give and receive. Reaching out is a natural process. However, reaching out to take or receive must be balanced with the act of giving. It is better to give than to receive, as the saying goes. Yes desire, seek, reach out, but carefully weigh the consequences.

God's gifts of life are there for the taking, but we must also learn to ask. Stealing by stealth will have its own punishment. Once we follow the path of God, eternal life is ours without having to steal it deceitfully.

The Lord God is described as, 'like one of us, knowing good and evil'. God is one who discerns good from evil. And only after this, is added, 'and live forever'. The priority matters and more so the description.

The Lord God is one not first and foremost who yields incredible eternal power. Not an Avengers superhero with strength beyond one's wildest imagination. The Lord God is, first and foremost, one who discerns, who has perfect conscious awareness, who sees, hears, knows and understands. The Lord God chooses good over evil, guides us towards truth and light. It is a Lord God who loves goodness over evil to the point of giving one's life.

> [35] And going a little farther, he threw himself on the ground and prayed that, if it were possible, the hour might pass from him. [36] He said, 'Abba, Father, for you all things are possible; remove this cup from me; yet, not what I want, but what you want'.
>
> Mark 14:35-36

A Lord God who has eternal life but is willing to offer all of life for the sake of knowing only good as opposed to evil. This is what makes our God most necessary in our lives. It is our God, a God with us, a God who understands what we go through and will be with us, guiding us to what is best. Yet this belief does not deny the fact that the choices between good and evil are precarious, difficult to discern and even harder to commit to.

The Lord God made us limited in knowledge and life, perhaps for our own good, and yet the ideal we should and do pursue is that of being like God. To be like God is to know good and evil, but it is to choose good. There is risk in creating humans but there is also hope and beauty when a human lives in the image of God.

The woman and man were tempted by unlimited knowledge. King Samuel also requests 'an understanding mind... able to discern between good and evil' but the two approaches are very different. Samuels's request is directed to God.

> ⁵At Gibeon the LORD appeared to Solomon in a dream by night; and God said, 'Ask what I should give you.' ⁶And Solomon said, 'You have shown great and steadfast love to your servant my father David, because he walked before you in faithfulness, in righteousness, and in uprightness of heart towards you; and you have kept for him this great and steadfast love, and have given him a son to sit on his throne today. ⁷And now, O LORD my God, you have made your servant king in place of my father David, although I am only a little child; I do not know how to go out or come in. ⁸And your servant is in the midst of the people whom you have chosen, a great people, so numerous they cannot be numbered or counted. ⁹Give your servant therefore an understanding mind to govern your people, able to discern between good and evil.'
>
> 1 Kings 3:5-9

Samuel requests this because he has recognised God's 'great and steadfast love' and has also recognised himself as 'I am only a little child'. Acknowledgment of the love bestowed on one and one's own need for blessings leads to true discernment of good and evil. For the first woman and man, things turned out very differently.

> **Genesis 3:23** *therefore the* Lord *God sent him forth from the garden of Eden, to till the ground from which he was taken.*

Let us take some time here to analyse a recurring theme in chapters two and three.

2:5 no one to till the ground

2:7 then the Lord God formed man

2:8 the Lord God planted a garden in Eden in the east; and there he put the man

2:15 the Lord God took the man and put him in the garden of Eden to till it and keep it

3:17 cursed is the ground because of you

3:23 therefore the Lord God sent him forth from the garden of Eden, to till the ground from which he was taken

The accounts repeatedly emphasise the delicate but necessary relationship between humans and the land. A land created but in need of constant attention, to be tilled and attended to. Humans disconnected from the land and their responsibilities results in difficulties. We are given a paradise that requires our ongoing attention, our tender love and care, but today we are so immersed in social media, virtual reality, gaming, etc. Where is the attention to exploration, the adventure, the outdoor enjoyments, the oneness with land, agriculture, walkabouts, gardens, National Parks and Reserves?

God placed humans to till the ground from which they were taken. A sort of restorative justice. The man was made from the ground but had strayed far. Only by returning to our original place do we remember who we really are. We are of the earth. We are meant 'to till the ground'. It is non-negotiable! Work is a necessity of life. Connection with the earth is vital to our survival. Whether in paradise or sent 'forth from the garden of Eden', the responsibility still remains 'to till the ground'.

To wait, at the mercy of the seasons, hoping that the rains will come and the sun will shine and the seeds will grow. We need to get out there and be tested. Life will call us out of our comfort zone. It needs to. We need to face struggle and hardship. We need to experience failure and disappointment, to appreciate life.

Despite the difficulties, there is much simple delight. The challenge of life will open our hearts, widen our minds, deepen our humility and draw out our appreciation.

The Lord God did not punish the man but simply reminded the man that he is human, that he must continue 'to till the ground from which he was taken' (3:23; 2:15). God has not changed. The man is the one who strayed, neglected his duties, desired other things, wanted to attain pomp, power and prestige, without the hard work. To be honest, at times one feels underqualified, not up to the task, lazy, certain to make a mess of things, uninterested, fearful of the task at hand. But there are no shortcuts. We all need to do the hard yards in order to appreciate life.

Whatever the attitude, life is about taking up the call to live responsibly not carelessly, fruitfully not lazily, committedly and not sluggishly. We are gifted with much beauty and pleasure but also the task to do more and be more and to live with purpose.

> From the place where we are right
> Flowers will never grow
> In the spring.
> The place where we are right
> Is hard and trampled
> Like a yard.
> But doubts and loves
> Dig up the world
> Like a mole, a plow.
> And a whisper will be heard in the place
> Where the ruined
> House once stood.
>
> Yehuda Amichai[88]

So the Lord God drove out the man, exiled east of the garden of Eden (3:24). 'East' is a metaphor for a new beginning. Yet it often feels in today's society that humans have driven out the Lord God. A godless society that has willingly turned its back and walked away for we will do things our way. Mature enough, knowledgeable enough,

---

[88] Yehuda Amichai, 'The Place Where We Are Right,' in the *Selected Poetry of Yehuda Amichai*, ed. and trans. Chana Bloch and Stephen Mitchell, (Oakland: University of California Press, 1996).

strong enough to live our lives, without having to lean on a higher authority to watch us, a divine presence to command us. The Lord God can stay in the garden of Eden, in blissful ignorance. Humans choose to be out in the wild, untamed, harsh world, to fight it out and make their own way.

To be in the garden or not, that is the question! We want the way of life of the garden of Eden and so we create day retreats, ecologically friendly accommodation, health regimes, mental wellbeing programs, yoga and spas, the leisurely lifestyle, organic sustenance, the softness of earth – we want holistic wellbeing – the buzz term today. Yes, we recreate our garden of Eden but we leave out God. Maybe the Lord God drove out humans, but we have not looked back! We instead play god and create a hollow image of what is. We seem to want a life without God. Maybe we are faithful agnostics, we may believe but do not bother us right now!

Genesis 3:24 *He drove out the man; and at the east of the garden of Eden he placed the cherubim, and a sword flaming and turning to guard the way to the tree of life.*

The Lord God focuses in the end of the chapter on 'the tree of life'. Earlier the Lord God created 'the tree of life... and the tree of the knowledge of good and evil' (3:9). There was no prohibition about the tree of life, only the tree of knowledge of good and evil (3:17), clearly commanding 'you shall not eat'. Now we have the Lord God placing 'a sword flaming and turning to guard the way to the tree of life'. In reading this verse, the cherubim specify where the divine Immanence was caused to dwell.

And have them make me a sanctuary, so that I may dwell among them. There I will meet you, and from above the mercy-seat, from between the two cherubim that are on the ark of the covenant, I will deliver to you all my commands for the Israelites.

Exodus 25:8, 22

(see also Exodus 29:45; Numbers 35:34; 1 Kings 6:13, 8:12, Ezekiel 43:7, 9)

The winged creature and the flashing sword are set to 'guard' (3:24) over the way to the tree of life. Human was placed in the garden of Eden to work it and to 'watch' it (2:15). In both instances, the root word is *shamar* (related to *shalom*) and it means to keep, guard, watch, or preserve. The winged creature and the flashing sword can just as easily, therefore, be understood, according to David James Stewart, as guarding and preserving the way back to the garden rather than preventing a return.[89]

The theology behind the text is the experience of exile from the garden that sets the stage for Israel's experience of the Babylonian exile. However, the exile is not the end of the story because there remains Eden, waiting. There is always a paradise to return to.

> 'Dear Sir,' I said – 'Although now long estranged,
> Man is not wholly lost nor wholly changed.
> Dis-graced he may be, yet is not de-throned,
> and keeps the rags of lordship once he owned:

---

[89] David James Stewart, 'The emergence of consciousness in Genesis 1–3: Jung's depth psychology and theological anthropology,' in Zygon, vol. 49, no. 2 (June 2014), pp 525-526.

Man, Sub-creator, the refracted Light
through whom is splintered from a single White
to many hues, and endlessly combined
in living shapes that move from mind to mind.'

J. R. R. Tolkien

The garden of Eden and the wilderness are not so far apart. In fact, they share the same boundaries. One lives in both worlds of the spiritual and the mundane, leisure and work, smooth sailing and difficulties.

We are not to fear the unknown, the out-there. And yet we are also not to forget the inner beauty and wonder. Mysticism and reality, spiritual and temporal, here and there, today and tomorrow, all intertwined. We cannot have one and not the other.

No matter how far out we stray, the garden of Eden always remains at the centre, the place from where we came and the place that awaits our return. The quest is to gain the knowledge of how to use one's experiences to live fully wherever we find ourselves. To erase the boundaries and delight in the whole.

And the Lord God goes with the woman and man out of the garden of Eden, for even the furthest away is still God's creation. The world is only possible with God.

Following on from the creation stories, the Lord God speaks on two separate occasions with Cain (4:6-7, 9-15), who is outside the garden of Eden, so the Lord God is now also located outside the garden. Indeed, it is only natural that God should abandon the garden of Eden after driving humans out. Never again in the Hebrew Bible is the garden of Eden referred to as an extant habitation of the Lord God. The Lord God decided to go wherever humans went. The serpent, incidentally, as Raanan Eichler reminds us, would remain free to slink into the withered and weed-filled garden whenever it felt impelled to sneak a bite from the tree of life.[90]

> We all know about being entitled
> And then growing careless.
> We all know about self-indulgence
> Even amid work to be done.
> We all know about being – for a moment
> Beyond Torah requirement and
> Outside of your world of command.
> We know about seasons of life not given
> Over to us
> And grief at being failed selves.
> We also know that you circle back among
> Us
> In harshness and in mercy
> In rigor and in generosity.
> Now our world has gone careless and
> Self-indulgent
> Beyond Torah.
> So circle back, we pray – one more time
> Among us with your mercy
> Our only source of comfort,
> For we belong to you in your
> Faithfulness.
>
> Walter Brueggeman, 'Circled by mercy'
> on reading 2 Samuel 1

---

[90] Eichler, 'When God Abandoned the Garden of Eden: A Forgotten Reading of Genesis 3:24', 31-32.

The way back home to paradise, to innocence, to goodness, is not easy, once lost. There are barriers that are put up against us, but we have the choice at 'new life' if we are prepared to fight our evil inclinations and to put our back to the grind, remembering that the garden's ethos remains binding on us.

The world is much more because we feel deep within us a need for goodness, for beauty, and we hope in the waiting, reaching out to the horizon and beyond. In the meantime, we fulfil our days which are wind-shaken and sun-drenched. Such is life. Morning and evening to be one with the world. We do not always experience paradise, but we have memory and God did create a 'very good' world.

And while we live our lives, the Lord God watches through the ages to await our homecoming with lasting patience. As God has always done, in this moment and forever, with longing and love.

Bibliography

Amichai, Yehuda. 'The Place Where We Are Right.' In the *Selected Poetry of Yehuda Amichai*, ed. and trans. Chana Bloch and Stephen Mitchell. Oakland: University of California Press, 1996.

Berry, Thomas. *The Sacred Universe. Earth, Spirituality, and Religion in the Twenty-First Century*. Edited by Mary Evelyn Tucker. New York: Columbia University Press, 2009.

———*The Dream of the Earth*, Berkeley: Counterpoint, 2015.

Bible Commentary. Produced by Theology of Work (TOW) Project. 'Genesis 1-11 and Work.' https://www.theologyofwork.org/old-testament/genesis-1-11-and-work

Brown, William P. 'Biblical Accounts of Creation.' In *The Old Testament and Ethics. A book-by-book survey*. Joel B. Green and Jacqueline E. Lapsley (Editors). Grand Rapids, Michigan: Baker Academic, 2013, (165-170).

_____ 'From Apology to Pedagogy: Interpreting the Bible Past and Present in the Seminary Classroom.' In *A Journal of Bible and Theology* 66(4), 2012: 371–382.

Carroll, James. *Christ Actually. The Son of God for the Secular Age*. London: William Collins, 2014.

Chilton, Bruce. 'Kingdom of God' in *The New Testament and Ethics. A Book-by-Book survey*. Joel B. Green, Editor. Grand Rapids, Michigan: Baker Academics, 2013, pp100-108.

Chittister, Joan. *The Monastic Way*, http://joanchittister.org/word-from-joan/monastic-way-0

Coleridge, Mark. *Words from the Wound*. Strathfield, NSW: St Pauls Publications, 2014.

de Chardin, Pierre Teilhard. *Christianity and Evolution*. Translated by Rene Hague. London: A Harvest Book, 1969.

_____ 'Struggle Against the Multitude.' In *Writings in Time of War*. Translated René Hague, New York: Harper and Row, 1968.

de Menezes, Rui. *The Global Vision of the Hebrew Bible*. Mumbai: St Pauls, 2009.

Deane-Drummond, Celia. 'Living from the Sabbath: Developing and Ecological Theology in the Context of Biodiversity.' In *Biodiversity and Ecology as Interdisciplinary Challenge*.

Denis Edwards and Mark Worthing, Editors. Adelaide: ATF Press, 2004, (1-13).

Delio, Ilia. *Christ in Evolution.* Maryknoll, N.Y.: Orbis Books, 2013.

Dowling, Jane N. *Come Forward! Bold enough to heal. A Spiritual Handbook for survivors of sexual abuse using Scripture, Visualisation and Art Therapy.* Victoria, Australia: Coventry Press, 2019.

Dumbrell, William J. *Covenant and Creation. An Old Testament Covenant Theology.* Milton Keynes: Paternoster, 2013.

Edwards, Denis. *Ecology at the Heart of Faith.* Maryknoll, New York: Orbis Books, 2006.

_____ *Jesus and the Cosmos.* Mahwah, New Jersey: Paulist Press, 1991.

Eichler, Raanan. 'When God Abandoned the Garden of Eden: A Forgotten Reading of Genesis 3:24' in *Vetus Testamentum* 65 (2015) 20-32.

Gogol, Nikolai. *Dead Souls,* Penguin Classics, Part 2: Chapter 3: 208-210 https://en.wikisource.org/wiki/Dead_Souls—A_Poem/Book_Two/Chapter_III

Greene, Graham. *The Power and the Glory,* new edn. London: William Heinemann and Bodley Head, 1971.

Hattie, John and Klaus Zierer, *10 Mindframes for Visible Learning. Teaching for Success.* London: Routledge, 2018.

Haught, John F. 'Teilhard de Chardin: Action, Contemplation, and the Cosmos.' In *RadicalGrace*, April-June 2010, Vol 23, no.2.

Heaney, Seamus. 'Lightenings.' In *Seeing Things.* London: Faber, 2010.

Hess, Richard. 'Evidence for Equality in Genesis 1-3.' In *Christians for Biblical Equality International*, Autumn 2008, Vol 7, Issue 3.

Hughes, Gerard W. *God of Surprises.* London: Darton, Longman and Todd Ltd, 2003.

Keller, Timothy. *The Prodigal Prophet. Jonah and the mystery of God's mercy.* Great Britain: Hodder & Stoughton, 2018.

Martini, Carlo Maria. *On the Body. A Contemporary Theology of the Human Person.* Victoria: John Garratt Publishing, 2000.

McCabe O.P., Herbert. *God Matters.* London: Geoffrey Chapman, 1987.

Merton, Thomas. *New Seeds of Contemplation.* New York: A New Directions Book, 1972.

Meyers, Carol. *Rediscovering Eve: Ancient Israelite Women in Context*. New York: Oxford University Press, 2013.

Moberly, R. W. L. 'Genesis 2–3: Adam and Eve and "the Fall."' In *The Theology of the Book of Genesis*. Cambridge Books Online, Cambridge University Press, 2009.

Olsen, Dennis T. 'Pentateuch' in *The Old Testament and Ethics. A book-by-book survey,*' Joel B. Green and Jacqueline E. Lapsley, editors (Grand Rapids: Michigan: Baker Academic, 2013.

Parker, Julie Faith. 'Blaming Eve Alone: Translation, Omission, and Implications of הַמָּע in Genesis 3:6b' in *Journal of Biblical Literature*, Vol. 132, No. 4 (2013), pp. 729-747.

Pope Francis. Plenary Session of The Pontifical Academy of Sciences. *Address of His Holiness Pope Francis on the Occasion of the Inauguration of The Bust in Honour of Pope Benedict XVI* Monday, 27 October 2014 https://w2.vatican.va/content/francesco/en/speeches/2014/october/documents/papa-francesco_20141027_plenaria-accademia-scienze.html

_____ Encyclical on Climate Change 2015 *Laudato Si'* (*Praise be to you my Lord*). http://m.vatican.va/content/francescomobile/en/encyclicals/documents/papa-francesco_20150524_enciclica-laudato-si.html

_____ *General Audience*, Wednesday, 17 May 2017. http://w2.vatican.va/content/francesco/en/audiences/2017/documents/papa-francesco_20170517_udienza-generale.html

_____ LII World Communications Day, 2018 http://www.vatican.va/content/francesco/en/messages/communications/documents/papa-francesco_20180124_messaggio-comunicazioni-sociali.html

Radcliffe O.P., Timothy. *Alive in God. A Christian Imagination*. London: Bloomsbury Continuum, 2019.

Ratzinger, Cardinal Joseph. *In the Beginning... A Catholic Understanding of the Story of Creation and the Fall*, Translated by Boniface Ramsey, O.P. Grand Rapids, Michigan: William B. Eerdmans Publishing Company, 1986.

Reid, Barbara E. *Wisdom's Feast. An Invitation to Feminist Interpretation of the Scriptures*. Grand Rapids, Michigan: William B. Eerdmans Publishing Company, 2016.

Rohr, Richard. *Dancing Standing Still. Healing the world from a place of prayer*, (New York: Paulist Press, 2014).

Sacks, Rabbi Jonathan. 'Three Stages of Creation - Covenant & Conversation – Parshah.' https://www.chabad.org/parshah/article_cdo/aid/4158654/jewish/Three-Stages-of-Creation.htm

_____ *Covenant & Conversation. The Genesis of Love* (Bereishit 5780), 23 October, 2019 https://rabbisacks.org/wp-content/uploads/2019/10/CC-5780-The-Genesis-of-Love-Bereishit-5780-2.pdf

_____ *Covenant and Conversation: A weekly reading of the Jewish Bible. Genesis: The Book of Beginnings*. New Milford, USA: Maggid Books, 2009.

Silf, Margaret. *The other side of chaos. Breaking through when life is breaking down*. Chicago: Loyola Press, 2011.

Smith, Julien C. H. and T. Laine Scales, 'Stewardship: A Biblical Model for the Formation of Christian Scholars.' In *JECB* 17:1 (2013), 79-97.

Smith, Mark S. 'Before Human Sin and Evil: Desire and Fear in the Garden of God.' In *The Catholic Biblical Quarterly*, Vol. 80, 2018:215-230.

Spufford, Francis. *Unapologetic: Why, Despite Everything, Christianity can still make a surprising emotional sense*. London: Faber, 2012.

Stewart, David James. 'The emergence of consciousness in Genesis 1-3: Jung's depth psychology and theological anthropology.' In *Zygon*, vol. 49, no. 2 (June 2014), pp. 509-529.

Sweet, Leonard and Frank Viola. *Jesus. A Theography*. Nashville: Thomas Nelson, 2012.

Swimme, Brian. *The Hidden Heart of the Cosmos: Humanity and the New Story*, Maryknoll: Orbis Books, 1996.

Swimme, Brian and Thomas Berry, *The Universe Story: From the Primordial Flaring Forth to the Ecozoic Era - A Celebration of the Unfolding of the Cosmos*, San Francisco: HarperSanFrancisco, 1992.

Tillich, Paul. *The Courage to Be*. London: Yale University Press, 2000.

Varengo, Peter. *You are the Kingdom. An exploration of discipleship through the Gospel imagery of the Kingdom as Divine Presence in the World*. Victoria, Australia: Coventry Press, 2020.

Walker-Jones, Arthur. 'Naming the human animal: Genesis 1-3 and other animals in human becoming' in *Zygon*, Vol. 52, no. 4, (December 2017), pp. 1005-1027.

Warner, Megan. "Therefore a Man Leaves His Father and His Mother and Clings to His Wife": Marriage and Intermarriage in Genesis 2:24 in *Journal of Biblical Literature*, Vol. 136, No. 2 (Summer 2017), pp. 269-288.

www.ingramcontent.com/pod-product-compliance
Lightning Source LLC
Chambersburg PA
CBHW011316080526
44588CB00020B/2730